The Development Dimension

Development Assistance Committee Members and Civil Society

OECD

BETTER POLICIES FOR BETTER LIVES

This work is published under the responsibility of the Secretary-General of the OECD. The opinions expressed and arguments employed herein do not necessarily reflect the official views of OECD member countries.

This document, as well as any data and map included herein, are without prejudice to the status of or sovereignty over any territory, to the delimitation of international frontiers and boundaries and to the name of any territory, city or area.

Please cite this publication as:
OECD (2020), *Development Assistance Committee Members and Civil Society*, The Development Dimension, OECD Publishing, Paris, *https://doi.org/10.1787/51eb6df1-en*.

ISBN 978-92-64-64815-9 (print)
ISBN 978-92-64-50083-9 (pdf)

The Development Dimension
ISSN 1990-1380 (print)
ISSN 1990-1372 (online)

Foreword

Agenda 2030 is clear on the need to engage civil society organisations (CSOs) in implementing and monitoring the Sustainable Development Goals. Given their capacity to bring the voices of those on the frontlines of poverty, inequality and vulnerability into development processes, CSOs have a particular role to play in ensuring no one is left behind. The Global Partnership for Effective Development Co-operation has committed to providing enabling environments for CSOs, both as implementing partners for members of the Development Assistance Committee (DAC) and as independent development actors in their own right. How DAC members work with civil society is part of CSO enabling environments.

Yet evidence from the Global Partnership monitoring, from CSOs' reporting of their day-to-day experience, and from observers and experts worldwide points to the need for much greater individual and collective effort to promote and protect enabling environments for civil society so that this sector's contribution to development can be maximised.

In this context, the OECD Development Co-operation Directorate (DCD) in 2017 established a work stream on civil society to provide guidance on DAC members' support for and engagement with civil society. This study, *Development Assistance Committee Members and Civil Society*, is a product of the work stream and identifies how DAC members are supporting and engaging with civil society and CSOs in DAC member and partner countries.

This study provides the most comprehensive review of DAC members' work with civil society ever undertaken by the OECD. It builds on the 2012 OECD guidance, *Partnering with Civil Society: 12 Lessons from Peer Reviews*, which has served as a reference point for members and their civil society partners. This study is rich with both qualitative and quantitative data from varied sources. Critical quantitative data were sourced from OECD statistics on official development assistance flows for CSOs. Literature, policies, reports and evaluations regarding DAC members' support for and engagement with CSOs inform the study. A key source of data is the findings of two separate but related surveys designed with input from an informal reference group of DAC members, CSOs and academics. A large-scale survey of DAC members was issued and all DAC members that financially support CSOs responded to it. A selection of CSO networks responded to a smaller-scale survey. Survey findings provided the basis for a working paper presented at the International Conference on Civil Society Space as part of the first OECD Civil Society Days in June 2019, co-organised with the Task Team on CSO Development Effectiveness and Enabling Environment.

The current study builds on that working paper, incorporating insights and feedback received at critical points during the study's development. Consultations with DAC members included meetings in 2018 of a group of DAC member experts (International Donor Group on Civil Society) and workshops in 2019 with the newly launched DAC Community of Practice on Civil Society. In keeping with the Framework for Dialogue between the DAC and Civil Society Organisations, consultations with CSOs from within and outside of the DAC-CSO Reference Group took place in 2019 under the auspices of the OECD Civil Society Days. Both DAC members and CSOs provided further input via online consultations in August and September 2019.

This study finds that DAC members are making efforts towards the type of support and engagement that enable CSOs to maximise their contribution to development, but that gaps remain between the aspiration of enabling civil society through effective development co-operation and members' CSO-related policies and practices. The intent is now to move from evidence gathering to policy action. In this vein, the DCD will continue on this collaborative and consultative path to provide support for DAC members to strengthen the promotion of enabling environments for civil society through DAC members' policies and practices. Chapter 3 of this study thus contains action points for further discussion with DAC members and CSOs and with others such as non-DAC member governments, foundations and academia. These ultimately are to be developed into a guidance document or a recommendation beginning in 2020.

Acknowledgements

Development Assistance Committee Members and Civil Society was prepared by the OECD Development Co-operation Directorate (DCD) under the leadership of Director Jorge Moreira da Silva. Jacqueline Wood, Team Lead and Senior Civil Society Specialist of the DCD's Foresight, Outreach and Policy Reform Unit (FOR), is the author of this study. Strategic guidance and oversight were provided by FOR Manager Ana Fernandes and Karin Fällman (formerly of FOR).

Thanks are extended to the multi-stakeholder informal reference group and the International Donor Group on Civil Society for their contributions to the survey design. Enormous appreciation is also extended to all members of the Development Assistance Committee (DAC), including the DAC Community of Practice on Civil Society, and of the DAC-CSO Reference Group who completed the How DAC Members Work with Civil Society surveys and provided inputs through in-person and online consultations.

The contributions at various stages of the study from within the OECD have been invaluable. Contributors include Marilyn Cham (DCD/FOR); Jenny Hedman (DCD/Global Partnerships and Policy); Ida McDonnell (DCD/Reviews, Results, Evaluations and Development Innovation); Henri-Bernard Solignac-Lecomte (DEV/Communications); Stacey Bradbury (DCD/Communications); Sara Casadevall Bellés (formerly DCD/Communications); Lance Cooper (DCD/Communications); Hugh MacLeman (DCD/Global Partnerships and Policy); Lisa Williams (DCD/Global Partnerships and Policy); Felix Zimmerman (DEV/Networks, Partnership and Gender); Alessandro Bellantoni (GOV/Governance Reviews and Partnerships); and Holly Richards (formerly PAC/Public Affairs and Media). Olivier Bouret (DCD/Financing for Sustainable Development) compiled OECD statistics. Susan Sachs edited the study. The French version was translated by the OECD translation division. The OECD's Public Affairs and Communications Directorate produced the publication. Publication of this study is possible thanks to financial support from the Swedish International Development Cooperation Agency.

Table of contents

FIGURES

INFOGRAPHICS

TABLES

Follow OECD Publications on:

 http://twitter.com/OECD_Pubs

http://www.facebook.com/OECDPublications

 http://www.linkedin.com/groups/OECD-Publications-4645871

http://www.youtube.com/oecdilibrary

http://www.oecd.org/oecddirect/

This book has...

 **StatLinks**

A service that delivers Excel® files from the printed page!

Look for the *StatLinks* at the bottom of the tables or graphs in this book. To download the matching Excel® spreadsheet, just type the link into your Internet browser, starting with the *http://dx.doi.org* prefix, or click on the link from the e-book edition.

Abbreviations and acronyms

ADA	Austrian Development Agency
AECID	Spanish Agency for International Development Cooperation (Agencia Española de Cooperación Internacional para el Desarrollo)
AFD	French Development Agency (Agence Française de Développement)
BMZ	Federal Ministry for Economic Cooperation and Development (Germany)
Camões	Portugese Institute for Cooperation and Language (Instituto da Cooperação e da Língua)
CLA	Collaborating, learning and adapting
CRS	Creditor Reporting System
CSO	Civil society organisation
DAC	Development Assistance Committee
DCD	Development Co-operation Directorate
DFAT	Department of Foreign Affairs and Trade (Australia)
DFID	Department for International Development (United Kingdom)
EC	European Commission
EU	European Union
GenderNet	DAC Network on Gender Equality
GIZ	Deutsche Gesellschaft für Internationale Zusammenarbeit (Germany)
GPEDC	Global Partnership for Effective Development Co-operation
IATI	International Aid Transparency Initiative
INCAF	International Network on Conflict and Fragility
JICA	Japan International Cooperation Agency
MFEA	Ministry of Foreign and European Affairs (Slovak Republic)
MEAE	Ministry for Europe and Foreign Affairs (France)
MFAIC	Ministry of Foreign Affairs and International Cooperation (Italy)
Norad	Norwegian Agency for Development Cooperation
ODA	Official development assistance

OECD	Organisation for Economic Co-operation and Development
OGP	Open Government Partnership
RBM	Results-based management
SAIDC	Slovak Agency for International Development Cooperation
SDC	Swiss Agency for Development and Cooperation
SDG	Sustainable Development Goal
Sida	Swedish International Development Cooperation Agency
UN	United Nations
USAID	United States Agency for International Development

Executive summary

The 2030 Agenda for Sustainable Development is clear on the need to mobilise civil society organisations (CSOs) to implement and uphold accountability for progress towards the Sustainable Development Goals. CSOs fill critical roles. They provide services in development and humanitarian situations, influence policies through dialogue and advocacy, and promote and protect human rights and democratisation. Their ability to reach people on the frontlines of poverty, inequality and vulnerability make them integral to fulfilling the 2030 Agenda promise to leave no one behind. CSOs are important to development co-operation, both as independent development actors and as implementing partners on behalf of members of the OECD Development Assistance Committee (DAC). According to OECD statistics, DAC members (hereinafter "members") allocated nearly USD 21 billion for CSOs in 2018, amounting to 15% of total bilateral aid.

Members have committed to providing and promoting enabling environments for civil society, including by ensuring that their work with civil society and the CSOs in it is effective. Yet evidence indicates that more must be done to provide and promote enabling environments. Around the world, legal and regulatory frameworks are being used to shrink civic space, limiting the possibilities for people to come together to improve lives. At the same time, there are gaps in CSOs' effectiveness and accountability. Donors, including members, struggle to appropriately leverage CSOs' knowledge, capabilities and influential role as public advocates for sustainable development, and they struggle to offer effective support for CSOs.

Building on key findings from surveys of and consultations with members and CSOs, *Development Assistance Committee Members and Civil Society* presents action points for members and the OECD DAC to make members' support for and engagement with CSOs and civil society more effective.

Key findings

- There is commonality in member definitions of CSOs, but also differences that may impede coherence of member actions.
- Most members have a policy document that covers their work with CSOs and civil society and is contained in either legislation, policies, strategies, guidelines, principles or action plans. About half have a civil society or CSO-specific policy document.
- CSOs call for greater integration of civil society considerations across a wide range of member policies.
- Most members have at least two types of objectives: to strengthen a pluralist and independent civil society in partner countries and to meet other development objectives beyond strengthening civil society in partner countries.
- Members more frequently cite the advantages rather than disadvantages of working with CSOs. Members also more frequently cite advantages of member country or international CSOs than of working with partner country CSOs.
- Members provide more financial support as project and/or programme support *through* CSOs than as partnership, framework and core support *to* CSO. Such support is considered better suited to

demonstrating tangible development results in the short term. CSOs experience members' financial support as short-term, overly directive and conditioned on member-defined priorities.

- A disproportionate amount of member funding is allocated to member country and international CSOs relative to partner country CSOs. Among the reasons cited for favouring these CSOs are members' legal or administrative requirements; transaction cost considerations; these CSOs' experience, including in demonstrating results; and their role in public awareness raising. Member funding also tends to flow to formal CSOs rather than extending to broader civil society.

- Systematic dialogue with CSOs is much more common at headquarters level than at partner country level. Dialogue does not necessarily meet good practice standards such as inclusivity, joint agenda setting, co-ordination among members, accessibility and timelines.

- CSOs and members continue to experience the administrative requirements and transaction costs associated with accessing and reporting on member funding as overly burdensome. Meeting these requirements means CSOs divert resources from their core work and the achievement of development results.

- Members are adopting more iterative and adaptive approaches to monitoring in growing recognition that inflexible application of results-based management that is focused on quick-win, quantitative and linear results can undermine CSOs' ability to innovate, take risks, be flexible and responsive to partners and situations on the ground, and address complex development problems towards long-term, transformative and sustainable change.

- Members encourage CSOs to foster relationships of greater accountability in partner countries, but do not adequately assess how the emphasis on upward accountability to members in their policies and practices may undermine CSO accountability at partner country level. While members are increasingly transparent about their financial flows to CSOs, the information is not always readily accessible to partner country stakeholders or disaggregated by partner country.

Based on these findings, this study offers the following action points for DAC members and the OECD DAC for improving their support for and engagement with CSOs and civil society.

Action points for DAC members

- Clarify definitions of CSOs and civil society towards establishing a common understanding across members and more broadly recognising civil society's diversity.

- In consultation with CSOs, develop policies that address both the member's objectives and ways of working with CSOs and civil society and contextual issues including civic space. Integrate civil society considerations across policy realms other than development co-operation.

- Embrace the two types of objectives for working with CSOs and civil society: to strengthen a pluralist and independent civil society in partner countries and to meet other development objectives beyond strengthening civil society in partner countries.

- Use a variety of strategies to rectify the imbalance between project/programme support and flows *through* CSOs as programme implementers on behalf of members, on one hand, and partnership/framework/core support and flows *to* CSOs as independent development actors, on the other.

- Augment direct financial support for partner country CSOs and support for a broader swathe of civil society including for more fluid and informal forms of association, new types of associations, and traditional civic actors.

- Make dialogue and consultation with CSOs and civil society more systematic and place greater emphasis on systematic dialogue at partner country level, while paying attention to good practice.

Encourage dialogue on policy realms other than development co-operation, such as on members' foreign policy and private sector investment and trade policies.

- Assess, minimise and monitor the transaction cost burden of members' administrative requirements, including by co-ordinating and harmonising requirements with other members based on the 2013 Code of Practice on Donor Harmonisation.
- Work with CSOs to define relevant, locally owned results frameworks and indicators while applying iterative and adaptive approaches to results management. Explore results indicators for strengthening a pluralist and independent civil society in partner countries.
- Support CSOs' accountability in partner countries using a mix of methods, while also enhancing member transparency and ensuring that member practices for working with CSOs and civil society do no harm to CSOs' partner country-level accountability.

Action points for the OECD DAC

- Develop up-to-date guidance on how members should work with CSOs and civil society or issue a recommendation for greater enforcement potential.
- Initiate discussion with members on the DAC reporting directives that pertain to definitions of civil society and CSOs and on the usefulness and accuracy of *to* and *through* coding of financial flows for CSOs.

The action points are offered for further discussion among members and CSOs, with a view to ultimately develop these action points – in consultation with members, CSOs and others beginning in 2020 – into a guidance or a recommendation for how members can more effectively work with civil society and, by extension, can improve enabling environments for civil society.

DAC SUPPORT TO CSOs IN NUMBERS

Figures from 2018

DAC members allocated **USD 21 billion - 15%** of total bilateral **ODA**	**Member country and international CSOs** receive a **disproportionate amount of funding (93%)**	Of **DAC support** for CSOs, **85%** goes **THROUGH CSOs** as implementers of **DAC members' projects**	**15%** goes **TO CSOs** to support them as **independent development actors**	**Member country CSOs** contribute an estimated **USD 42 billion** in private contributions to **development co-operation**

WHAT'S WORKING WELL

✓ Members appreciate CSOs' **on-the-ground knowledge**, proximity to **beneficiaries** and ability to reach **vulnerable and marginalised people**, critical to the SDGs and leaving no one behind.

✓ Most members' objectives for working with CSOs include **strengthening civil society** in developing countries, and **implementing members' projects.**

✓ **Systematic dialogue** between **members and CSOs** is on the rise, especially at **headquarters level.**

✓ Some members are making efforts to **streamline administrative requirements** and implement flexible, learning-oriented **results management.**

WAYS TO WORK BETTER

→ OBJECTIVES	→ FUNDING	→ ADMINISTRATION AND RESULTS MANAGEMENT	→ IN DEVELOPING COUNTRIES
Reflect not only the **instrumental value of CSOs as implementers**, but also the **intrinsic value** of a **strong, pluralist** and **independent civil society.**	**Improve coherence** between objectives and ways of working with CSOs by **rectifying the imbalance** between **support through and to CSOs** and other methods.	**Streamline and harmonise administrative requirements** and adopt adaptive, flexible, learning-oriented **results management.**	**Expand funding** and **dialogue** to developing country CSOs and a wider swathe of **civil society actors.**

Work together to develop OECD DAC guidance or a recommendation to improve how members work with CSOs.

Overview: Enabling civil society through effective development co-operation

Development Assistance Committee members, recognising the important development role of civil society, channel nearly USD 21 billion, or 15% of all bilateral official development assistance, to civil society organisations (CSOs). To ensure they are effectively supporting CSOs as part of enabling environments for civil society, members should clarify their civil society policies, ease the administrative burden on CSOs, and enhance CSOs' legitimacy and accountability through less rigid steering of funds and programmes. This Overview of data, survey responses and relevant literature evaluates the current state of member-CSO relations and presents action points to further improve them.

Civil society and the civil society organisations (CSOs) in it are important development actors. CSOs fill roles as providers of services in development and humanitarian situations. They contribute to policy development through dialogue and advocacy. They are leaders in the promotion and protection of human rights and democratisation. CSOs are appreciated for their experience, expertise, and quick and flexible response. They are also valued for their ability to identify new as well as longstanding and often systemic obstacles to social, economic and democratic development and for their capacity to innovate, elaborate and implement solutions.

CSOs are important to development co-operation, both as development actors in their own right and as implementing partners for members of the OECD Development Assistance Committee (DAC). Statistics from the OECD show that in 2018, DAC members (hereinafter "members") allocated almost USD 21 billion for CSOs, amounting to 15% of total bilateral official development assistance (ODA) (OECD, 2020[1]). Member country CSOs also bring considerable privately sourced contributions, estimated at USD 42 billion in 2018, to development co-operation (OECD, 2020[1]).

The significance of CSOs in development is widely recognised. The 2030 Agenda for Sustainable Development is clear on the need for all development actors inclusive of CSOs to engage in implementation and monitoring of the Sustainable Development Goals (SDGs). The strengthened global partnership for achievement of SDG 17 (revitalize the global partnership for sustainable development) is meant to involve all levels of government, the private sector and civil society, among others, in a whole-of-society approach to SDG achievement. Further, CSOs play a crucial role in facilitating people's participation and the pursuit of accountability. In this sense, they also are critical to achieving SDG 16 (promote just, peaceful and inclusive societies) and are part and parcel of such societies and the accountable institutions called for in this SDG. The 2018 OECD report, *Development Co-operation Report, Joining Forces to Leave No One Behind*, highlights the vital role of CSOs in bringing the voices of those on the frontlines of poverty, inequality and vulnerability into development processes and thus in helping to meet the 2030 Agenda promise to leave no one behind (OECD, 2018[2]). In addition, the Grand Bargain sees CSOs as key partners in relation to humanitarian action and commits Grand Bargain adherents to work with CSOs effectively and efficiently (Inter-Agency Standing Committee, 2019[3]).

Since the 2008 High Level Forum on Aid Effectiveness, the multi-stakeholder constituency of the Global Partnership for Effective Development Co-operation (GPEDC) fully acknowledges the development role of CSOs, both as implementing partners of development co-operation providers, partner country governments and the private sector and as independent development actors in their own right (OECD, 2008[4]). The GPEDC – inclusive of members and other development co-operation providers as well as partner country governments, CSOs and others – also recognises that enabling environments are necessary if CSOs are to maximise their contributions to development. At the high level and senior level meetings in 2016 and 2019, the GPEDC reaffirmed commitments to provide enabling environments for CSOs and to promote CSOs' development effectiveness (GPEDC, 2016[5]; GPEDC, 2019[6]). The GPEDC monitoring framework reflects these commitments in its Indicator 2, which assesses enabling environments for civil society in terms of the presence of space for CSOs in policy dialogue; effective support for and engagement with CSOs by official development co-operation providers; enabling legal and regulatory frameworks for CSOs; and effective, accountable and transparent CSOs (GPEDC, 2018[7]).

Nonetheless, evidence indicates more must be done to create and protect enabling environments for CSOs and civil society (Task Team on CSO Development Effectiveness and Enabling Environment, 2014[8]; OECD/UNDP, 2016[9]; OECD/UNDP, 2019[10]; Brechenmacher and Carothers, 2019[11]). Around the world, efforts by various governments to restrict the legal, regulatory and policy space (also called civic space) in which civil society operates have grown. Increasingly, governments are using laws, policies and practices to limit the possibilities for people to come together to improve their everyday lives. At the same time, there remain gaps in CSOs' effectiveness and accountability and concerns about their legitimacy, their results, and the challenges to co-ordination among CSOs and with governments. While there is considerable scope for members to leverage CSOs' knowledge, capabilities and influential role as public advocates for sustainable development, members do not yet appear to be offering effective development support for CSOs as part of the enabling environment for civil society.

Development Assistance Committee Members and Civil Society provides a comprehensive review of members' support for and engagement with civil society and the CSOs in it. The study finds that members are making efforts towards providing the type of support and engagement that would enable CSOs to maximise their contribution to development, but that members' policies and practices sometimes fall short. The study is a significant step to support members to reflect on how they can better work with civil society and CSOs in development.

This study is organised in three chapters and two annexes. Chapter 1 presents insights from existing OECD guidance and other relevant literature to draw out lessons and remaining challenges in this area. The main guidance reviewed is the 2012 publication, *Partnering with Civil Society: 12 Lessons from DAC Peer Reviews* (OECD, 2012[12]). This guidance in turn drew on an earlier overview entitled *How DAC Members Work with Civil Society Organisations* that is similar to, but less comprehensive than, this current study (OECD, 2011[13]). Chapter 2 reviews OECD statistics on official development assistance (ODA) flows for CSOs and discusses responses of members and CSOs to two separate surveys conducted over 2018 and 2019; members' policy documents that are relevant to their work with civil society; and insights and feedback from online and in-person consultations with both members and CSOs. Members and CSOs were consulted through the International Donor Group on Civil Society, the DAC Community of Practice on Civil Society and the DAC-CSO Reference Group. Preliminary Chapter 2 findings were previously published in a working paper (Wood and Fällman, 2019[14]). Chapter 3 presents action points for members and the OECD DAC to improve the effectiveness of members' support for and engagement with CSOs and civil society as part of providing enabling environments for civil society. The action points are offered for further discussion among members and CSOs, with a view to ultimately develop them into a guidance or a recommendation. Annex A contains additional information on this study's sources and research methods and Annex B presents data on financial flows for CSOs.

The remainder of this Overview summarises key findings from the Chapter 1 review of the literature and the 2012 OECD guidance and from the Chapter 2 review of the survey and consultation results. The findings pertain to definitions of CSOs and civil society; objectives for working with CSOs and civil society; advantages and disadvantages of working with CSOs; policies for working with CSOs and civil society; financial support mechanisms and recipients; approaches to dialogue and consultation; administrative requirements; monitoring and learning methods; and practices to promote accountability and transparency. The Overview concludes with action points for members and the OECD DAC itself to improve the effectiveness of their work with CSOs and civil society and, by extension, the enabling environment for civil society.

Key findings

Defining CSOs and civil society

Civil society is the collection of CSOs and other semi-formal and non-formal groupings through which people associate. Civil society is also a sphere or space in which CSOs and other groups interact with each other and with others. While there is commonality in member definitions of CSOs (and in definitions of non-governmental organisations or NGOs), there are also differences, especially in the degree to which the definitions reflect the diversity of civil society actors. Members rarely define civil society. Defining civil society and CSOs is not always straightforward because of the diversity of forms of organisation and association across the civil society sector. However, the absence of a common definition may impede member coherence in implementing the action points offered in this study. Additionally, member definitions of CSOs and civil society that are not broad and inclusive may prevent members from engaging with the range of formal and informal groupings that comprise the civil society sector. The OECD and DAC definitions of CSOs (and NGOs) are a good starting point towards greater commonality of definitions among members.

Policies for working with CSOs and civil society

The majority of members have some form of policy document that covers their work with CSOs and civil society, and approximately half of them have civil society or CSO-specific policy documents. The type of document that members consider to constitute their CSO or civil society policy varies and includes legislation, policies, strategies, guidelines, principles and action plans. Policies are generally developed, and sometimes also monitored, in consultation with CSOs. A CSO and/or civil society policy document is necessary to provide a transparent framework that articulates a member's objectives and ways of working with CSOs and civil society. In addition to calling for a CSO and/or civil society policy, CSOs call for greater integration of civil society considerations, including civic space issues, across a wide range of member country policies to strengthen policy coherence. Policy areas that would benefit from civil society-related coverage include foreign policy and policies on private sector investment, trade, migration, security, taxation and digital technology.

Objectives for working with CSOs and civil society

Members should clearly articulate their objectives for working with CSOs and civil society. Ideally, members have two types of objectives. One will reflect the intrinsic value of a strong, pluralist and independent civil society. The other reflects the instrumental value of CSOs as implementing partners on behalf of members to meet development objectives other than strengthening civil society and usually in specific sectors or themes (e.g. health, education, democratisation and gender). According to their survey responses, almost all members have multiple objectives for working with CSOs and civil society. A majority of members have at least the two aforementioned types of objectives. Significantly, members pursue the strengthening civil society objective using a variety of financial and non-financial practices to promote enabling environments for CSOs and civil society in partner countries. Public awareness raising in member countries is also an important objective for members. There is growing awareness among members that in fragile settings, their objectives should integrate comprehensive and complementary approaches that ultimately reduce needs, as is called for in the DAC Recommendation on the Humanitarian-Development-Peace Nexus (OECD DAC, 2019[15]).

Advantages and disadvantages of working with CSOs and civil society

Many members see many advantages of working with CSOs such as CSOs' proximity to beneficiaries, their ability to reach people in vulnerable situations or facing high risk of marginalisation, and their capacity to deliver services. At the same time, members experience some countervailing difficulties in working with CSOs such as duplication and lack of co-ordination and the challenge of demonstrating and aggregating results. On balance, however, the survey finds members more frequently cite the advantages rather than disadvantages of working with CSOs. Members also more frequently identify advantages of member country or international CSOs compared to those of working with partner country CSOs, though many advantages are nonetheless attributed to partner country CSOs. A significant and almost equal number of members ascribe the most frequently selected advantages of CSOs to both member country and international CSOs as well as to partner country CSOs, which suggests that each type of CSO has the potential to be valued partners for members. However, the ability of member country CSOs to raise public awareness and engage citizens on development issues in member countries is cited by members as a key advantage of member country or international CSOs but not of partner country CSOs.

How financial support is provided

The most commonly used mechanism of member financial support for CSOs is project and/or programme support. Partnership, framework and core support mechanisms are less commonly used by members. According to OECD statistics for 2018, most financial support for CSOs (85%) flows *through* CSOs as project/programme implementers on behalf of members, with the remaining 15% flowing *to* CSOs as independent development actors in the form of core support. A key reason members favour project/programme support *through* CSOs is that such support is deemed better suited to demonstrating tangible development results in the short term. Still, CSOs experience members' financial support as short-term and overly directive, with many conditions tied to member-defined priorities. Core support is CSOs' preferred type of support. It is also the most development-effective type of support, with advantages such as predictability, flexibility, sustainability, administrative efficiency, and, significantly, ownership and accountability. Whatever type of support is provided for CSOs, it must allow them to respond to the priorities and demands of their partners at partner country level. Rigid steering undermines CSOs' ability to do so, and thus is detrimental to CSOs' partner country-level legitimacy and accountability and may weaken rather than strengthen civil society in partner countries.

Members do pursue the objective of strengthening civil society in partner countries within their project/programme mechanisms and *through* support, for example with support that does not overly rigidly steer CSOs or that involves capacity development of partner country CSOs. Statistics on member flows *to* and *through* CSOs do not adequately assess the extent to which members are pursuing the objective of strengthening civil society in partner countries. More nuanced information on the design of members' mechanisms is needed to assess the match between objectives and type of support.

Who receives financial support

A disproportionate amount of member funding is allocated to member country or international CSOs relative to partner country CSOs, even though members cite many of the same advantages (and disadvantages) of working with member country or international CSOs that they cite regarding working with partner country CSOs. Members have a range of reasons for favouring member country or international CSOs. These include members' legal, regulatory and administrative requirements and, relatedly, transaction cost considerations such as limited member capacity to administer direct support for additional small and often (though not necessarily) less experienced partner country CSOs. Other reasons are the extensive experience and expertise of member country and international CSOs, including in demonstrating results, and their knowledge and networks. Member country CSOs also are preferred because they contribute to public awareness raising and citizen engagement at home; member country publics, in general, trust these CSOs; and they play a role in informal diplomacy abroad. The voice of these CSOs and member country publics also informs members' tendency to support member country CSOs.

Member funding also tends to flow to formal CSOs. This means that it may not extend to elements of the rich associational life that make up the broader civil society in both in member and partner countries, such as traditional forms of association (e.g. faith-based groups, trade unions, professional associations, etc.); the growing body of hybrid forms such as social enterprises; and more informal, fluid forms of civil society action that are on the rise. Some members are at the early stages of seeking to work with a wider diversity of civil society actors beyond formal CSOs, including through multi-donor pooled funds.

Dialogue and consultation with CSOs and civil society

All members engage CSOs in dialogue and consultation, with a majority using both systematic, advance-planned dialogue fora and dialogue on an ad hoc basis. Systematic dialogue with CSOs is much more common at headquarters level than at partner country level. Dialogue at partner country level tends to be ad hoc, with approximately one third of members not consulting with CSOs at partner country level at all.

Dialogue does not necessarily meet good practice standards such as inclusivity, joint agenda setting, accessibility and timelines or include feedback mechanisms on uptake (or not) of consultation inputs. Co-ordination of dialogue among members, particularly at partner country level, needs attention to avoid duplication of effort and over-burdening CSOs with consultation demands. CSOs assess they have capacity gaps to adequately participate in dialogue and consultations. At the same time, there are benefits to engaging CSOs in dialogue on topics other than members' development co-operation policies such as foreign policy, private sector investment and trade policies and towards greater relevance and coherence of member policies.

Administrative requirements

CSOs and members continue to experience the administrative requirements and transaction costs associated with accessing and reporting on member funding as overly burdensome. It can be challenging to change such requirements, as they are integral to members' domestic accountability to their governments, parliaments and public. To meet these requirements, however, CSOs divert valuable time and resources from their core work and the achievement of development results on the ground. Even when some members seek to streamline their administrative requirements to reduce the transaction cost burden through multi-year agreements, greater budget flexibility, simplified applications and other practices, CSOs find that new requirements cancel out such streamlining efforts. Some alignment with CSOs' own administrative systems and formats for proposals and reporting is occurring and there is some combining of CSO and member requirements and formats. Yet little in the way of harmonisation of member requirements is evident beyond member participation in multi-donor pooled funds, though these funds are only a partial solution. Members that participated in the Swedish International Development Cooperation Agency-led harmonisation initiative that created the 2013 Code of Practice on Donor Harmonisation (Sida, 2019, p. 26[16]) and associated tools have not followed up on implementing the Code.

Monitoring for results and learning

Monitoring is critical for both members and CSOs to demonstrate that ODA for CSOs is achieving development results. However, inflexible application of results-based management focused on quick-win or quantitative results and linear results chains can undermine CSOs' ability to innovate, take risks, be flexible and responsive to partners and situations on the ground, and address complex development problems towards long-term, transformative and sustainable change. Yet it is because of these capabilities that members choose to work with CSOs. Members are increasingly adopting more iterative and adaptive approaches to monitoring that are context-sensitive and better integrate learning and flexibility to inform decision making on implementation directions. Investment is needed in CSOs' capacity for results monitoring as members continue to adjust and improve their results management approaches.

A majority of members use agreements (or contracts) with CSOs that include some form of results framework with indicators as the basis for CSOs' monitoring and reporting of their initiatives. Approximately half of members allow CSOs to define or co-define all or some of the indicators. Use of CSO-defined indicators can help to promote relevance, ownership and local-level accountability and reduce the administrative burden on CSOs.

Accountability and transparency of CSOs and members

Their accountability, and perceptions of their accountability, are critical to CSOs' effectiveness as either independent development actors or programme implementers on behalf of members. CSOs tend to prioritise their relationship of upward accountability to members, although accountability of CSOs, and of members, at partner country level is integral to build and maintain CSOs' legitimacy in the partner country where they work. Members use multiple practices to encourage CSOs to foster relationships of greater accountability in partner countries that range from participatory approaches to encouraging CSO co-ordination and supporting CSO self-regulation mechanisms. However, members inadequately assess how the emphasis in their own policies and practices on upward accountability to members may undermine CSO accountability at partner country level. While members are increasingly transparent about their financial flows to CSOs, the information is not always readily accessible to partner country stakeholders or disaggregated by partner country. CSOs and members share responsibility for upholding accountability and transparency at partner country level, as these are essential leverage to counter the trend of restricting the space for civil society.

Based on these findings, this study offers the following action points for improving member support for and engagement with CSOs and civil society as part of an enabling environment. The action points for both members and the DAC itself update guidance provided in *Partnering with Civil Society: 12 Lessons from Peer Reviews*, the 2012 OECD report that has been the sole source of DAC guidance on the subject of working with civil society. The action points lay the groundwork for development of a new policy instrument in the form of a guidance or a recommendation on enabling environments for civil society.

Action points for DAC members

- Clarify definitions of CSOs and civil society towards a common understanding across members and greater inclusivity that reflects the diversity of forms of organising and associating across the civil society sector.

- Develop policy documents that address the member's objectives and ways of working with CSOs and civil society as well as contextual issues including civic space. Develop and monitor these policy documents in consultation with CSOs. Integrate civil society considerations including civic space issues across policy realms other than development co-operation that directly or indirectly affect CSOs and civil society.

- Embrace the two types of objectives for working with CSOs and civil society: to strengthen a pluralist and independent civil society in partner countries and to meet other development objectives beyond strengthening civil society in partner countries. Integrate promotion of enabling environments for civil society in partner countries into the strengthening civil society objective. Reflect the importance of complementary humanitarian, development and peace actions and the crucial role and contribution of civil society actors in these actions.

- Rectify the imbalance between project/programme support mechanisms and flows *through* CSOs as programme implementers on behalf of members, on one hand, and partnership/framework/core support mechanisms and flows *to* CSOs as independent development actors, on the other. Implement strategies to help rectify the imbalance, for example by minimising directive-ness and designing *through* support to meet the strengthening civil society in partner countries objective; increasing the availability of core support *to* CSOs; identifying ways to better demonstrate that strengthening a pluralist and independent civil society is a valuable development result; and maintaining multiple financial support mechanisms. Identify and rectify obstacles to incentivising more coherent humanitarian-development-peace approaches in financial support mechanisms.

- Augment direct financial support for partner country CSOs and support for a broader swathe of civil society, including for fluid or informal forms of association, new types of associations such as social enterprises, and traditional civic actors (e.g. professional associations, faith-based organisations and trade unions). Share lessons among members and with CSOs for tackling the reasons that funding tends to miss these CSOs and civil society actors.

- Make dialogue and consultation with CSOs and civil society more systematic and place greater emphasis on systematic dialogue at partner country level, while also maintaining opportunities for responsive, strategic and less formal ad hoc dialogue. Encourage dialogue between CSOs and members' representatives that are responsible for policy realms other than development co-operation such as members' foreign policy and private sector investment and trade policies and encourage dialogue between CSOs and partner country governments. Improve the quality and efficiency of dialogue with CSOs by following good practice, including co-ordination of dialogue among members.

- Assess, minimise and monitor the transaction cost burden of members' administrative requirements. Address the administrative burden, for example by shifting to strategic, streamlined requirements; using CSOs' own or co-defined formats and systems; using multi-year funding agreements; adapting requirements to contribution size and risk level; and co-ordinating and harmonising with other members such as through multi-donor pooled funds and other methods. Revisit the 2013 Code of Practice on Donor Harmonisation as a basis for action.

- Work collaboratively with CSOs to define results frameworks and indicators that are most relevant to the initiative at hand, the individuals and communities involved, and the changes (results) that CSOs and the individuals and communities they work with would like to see. Collaborate with CSOs to explore and experiment with results indicators for strengthening a pluralist and independent civil society in partner countries. Apply iterative and adaptive approaches to results management, with greater emphasis on learning to inform programming directions in an adaptive manner while investing in building CSOs' results monitoring and learning capacities.

- Use a mix of methods to support CSOs' accountability in partner countries, recognising this as essential to strengthening civil society and enabling environments. Assess and address how member practices for working with CSOs and civil society may undermine CSOs' legitimacy and accountability at partner country level and work towards ensuring that member practices do no harm to CSOs' partner country-level accountability. Enhance member transparency regarding funding for CSOs so funding is disaggregated by partner country and accessible to partner country stakeholders, using an appropriate level of accessibility so CSOs in sensitive environments are not put at risk.

Action points for the OECD DAC

- Develop up-to-date guidance on how members should work with CSOs and civil society or issue a recommendation for greater enforcement potential. Do so in collaboration and consultation with the OECD DAC Community of Practice on Civil Society and the DAC-CSO Reference Group. Apply an iterative, peer learning approach to implementation of the guidance or recommendation.

- Initiate discussion with members on the DAC reporting directives as regards definitions of civil society and CSOs and on the usefulness and accuracy of *to* and *through* coding of financial flows for CSOs.

All told, members appear to be making efforts to work with CSOs in ways that enable the CSOs to maximise their contribution to development. Each member should continuously examine and adapt its policies and practices to ensure development co-operation with CSOs is as effective as possible. Coherence between objectives and members' means of support for and engagement with CSOs is key.

References

Brechenmacher, S. and T. Carothers (2019), *Defending Civic Space: Is the International Community Stuck?*, Carnegie Endowment for International Peace, https://carnegieendowment.org/files/WP_Brechenmacker_Carothers_Civil_Space_FINAL.pdf. [11]

GPEDC (2019), *Co-Chairs' Statement - Senior Level Meeting of the Global Partnership for Effective Development Co-operation*, Global Partnership for Effective Development Co-operation (GPEDC), Paris, https://effectivecooperation.org/wp-content/uploads/2019/07/2019-Senior-Level-Meeting-Co-Chair-Statement.pdf. [6]

GPEDC (2018), *2018 Monitoring Guide for National Co-ordinators from Participating Governments*, Global Partnership for Effective Development Co-operation (GPEDC), Paris, http://effectivecooperation.org/pdf/2018_Monitoring_Guide_National_Coordinator.pdf. [7]

GPEDC (2016), *Nairobi Outcome Document*, Global Partnership for Effective Development Co-operation (GPEDC), Paris, http://effectivecooperation.org/wp-content/uploads/2016/12/OutcomeDocumentEnglish.pdf. [5]

Inter-Agency Standing Committee (2019), *The Grand Bargain: What is the Grand Bargain*, United Nations Office for the Coordination of Humanitarian Affairs, New York/Geneva, https://interagencystandingcommittee.org/system/files/gb_simplified_v4_july_2019.pdf (accessed on 23 August 2019). [3]

OECD (2020), *Creditor Reporting System (database)*, https://stats.oecd.org/Index.aspx?DataSetCode=crs1. [1]

OECD (2018), *Development Co-operation Report 2018: Joining Forces to Leave No One Behind*, OECD Publishing, Paris, https://dx.doi.org/10.1787/dcr-2018-en. [2]

OECD (2012), *Partnering with Civil Society: 12 Lessons from DAC Peer Reviews*, OECD Development Co-operation Peer Reviews, OECD Publishing, Paris, https://dx.doi.org/10.1787/9789264200173-en. [12]

OECD (2011), *How DAC Members Work with Civil Society Organisations: An Overview*, OECD Publishing, Paris, http://www.oecd.org/dac/peer-reviews/Final_How_DAC_members_work_with_CSOs_ENGLISH.pdf. [13]

OECD (2008), *Accra Agenda for Action*, OECD Publishing, Paris, https://dx.doi.org/10.1787/9789264098107-en. [4]

OECD DAC (2019), "DAC Recommendation on the Humanitarian-Development-Peace Nexus", OECD Publishing, Paris, https://legalinstruments.oecd.org/en/instruments/OECD-LEGAL-5019. [15]

OECD/UNDP (2019), *Making Development Co-operation More Effective: 2019 Progress Report*, OECD Publishing, Paris, https://doi.org/10.1787/26f2638f-en. [10]

OECD/UNDP (2016), *Making Development Co-operation More Effective: 2016 Progress Report*, OECD Publishing, Paris, https://doi.org/10.1787/9789264266261-en. [9]

Sida (2019), *Guiding Principles for Sida's Engagement with and Support to Civil Society*, Swedish International Development Cooperation Agency (Sida), Stockholm, https://www.sida.se/contentassets/86933109610e48929d76764121b63fc6/10202931_guiding_principle_2019_no_examples_web.pdf. [16]

Task Team on CSO Development Effectiveness and Enabling Environment (2014), *Review of Evidence: Progress on Civil Society-related Commitments of the Busan High Level Forum*, https://taskteamcso.com/wp-content/uploads/2019/04/Task-Team-Review-of-Evidence.pdf. [8]

Wood, J. and K. Fällman (2019), "Enabling civil society: Select survey findings", *OECD Development Co-operation Working Papers*, No. 57, OECD Publishing, Paris, https://dx.doi.org/10.1787/54903a6a-en. [14]

1 What the literature says about civil society and Development Assistance Committee members

This chapter provides a framework for understanding how OECD DAC members work with civil society and civil society organisations (CSOs). It reviews existing OECD guidance, chiefly the 2012 report, *Partnering with Civil Society: 12 Lessons from DAC Peer Reviews*, and presents insights from relevant literature and lessons. The chapter first discusses definitions applied to the diverse civil society sector. It then explores existing guidance and remaining challenges around members' policies, objectives, financial support mechanisms, administrative requirements, monitoring, accountability and transparency in their relations with civil society. Throughout, the chapter highlights areas where additional, stronger and more nuanced emphasis can reinforce these important relationships.

1.1. Introduction: Civil society organisations in development co-operation

Civil society organisations (CSOs) have long been part of the domestic landscape of many countries that are OECD Development Assistance Committee (DAC) members and where they contribute to social, economic, cultural and democratic development. The economic contribution of CSOs in member countries is estimated at 5% of gross domestic product, a share equal to that of major industries (Salamon, 2010, p. 198[1]).

CSOs have played a role in development co-operation for as long as such co-operation has existed. In 2018, DAC members (hereinafter "members") allocated nearly USD 21 billion for CSOs (OECD, 2020[2]). The share of total bilateral aid that members allocate for CSOs has remained fairly steady. While this share decreased slightly, from 16% in 2010 to 15% in 2018, the USD 21 billion allocated in 2018 is an 11% increase in real terms over 2010 (OECD, 2020[2]).[1] This figure alone shows that CSOs' significance in development co-operation cannot be underestimated.

CSOs also raise considerable financial resources for development. According to OECD figures, CSOs in member countries raised at least USD 42 billion in private contributions to development co-operation in 2018, representing approximately 30% of members' total bilateral aid (OECD, 2020[2]).[2]

The contribution of CSOs to development co-operation is not exclusively a financial one. Civil society and the CSOs in it are important agents of change. They provide a means for people's expression, enable people to claim their rights and promote rights-based approaches, shape and oversee development policies, and provide services complementary to those provided by governments (OECD, 2011, p. 6[3]). Moreover, they are valued for their knowledge, experience and expertise; their agility in responding to changing needs and contexts; and their cost-effectiveness (Hulme and Edwards, 1997[4]). They are seen to be adept at identifying new or longstanding obstacles to development that might otherwise be ignored by governments and at devising strategies to address these (OECD, 2010, p. 27[5]). Their connections to people on the frontlines of poverty, inequality and vulnerability, and their ability to channel these voices into development processes, are considered a critical asset to help meet the 2030 Agenda for Sustainable Development promise to leave no one behind (Bushan et al., 2018[6]).

Indeed, the 2030 Agenda clearly calls for CSO engagement in implementation of the Sustainable Development Goals (SDGs). CSOs, among other actors, are required for the whole-of-society approach to SDG achievement. Their important role is especially embodied in SDG 17, which is to strengthen the means of implementation and revitalise the global partnership for sustainable development. CSO engagement is also a cornerstone of the peaceful and inclusive societies and accountable and inclusive institutions called for in SDG 16.

CSO engagement in the SDGs requires enabling conditions to be in place. The multi-stakeholder constituency of the Global Partnership for Effective Development Co-operation (GPEDC), which includes members of the DAC as well as CSOs, has committed to provide such conditions (also referred to as enabling environments for CSOs) and to promote CSOs' own effectiveness and accountability, all as key components of effectiveness.[3]

For these reasons, it is in the interest of members, as well as in the interest of CSOs and the individuals and communities whose lives development co-operation seeks to improve, to ensure that members' work with CSOs enables such organisations to maximise their contribution to development.

1.2. Defining civil society and CSOs

Existing guidance

The OECD (2012[7]) report, *Partnering with Civil Society: 12 Lessons from DAC Peer Reviews*, is a reference point for the discussion in this chapter of what the literature says. The guidance draws on peer reviews as well as surveys of and consultations with members and CSOs and presents a number of recommendations for members. Its intent is to guide members in designing and implementing good policies and practices for their work with civil society. Since its publication, *Partnering with Civil Society* has been the singular source of DAC guidance on the subject of working with civil society, complemented by peer reviews.

This study also draws on surveys and consultations undertaken with members and CSOs.[4] Considered together with elements of the OECD guidance, these point to several areas that need continued attention from members, among them definitions of civil society and CSOs, policies, objectives, financial support mechanisms and recipients, dialogue, administrative requirements, monitoring and evaluation, and accountability and transparency.

One of the *Partnering with Civil Society* recommendations (lesson 4) is that members build on current definitions and knowledge of civil society to agree on and use common terminology regarding CSOs and development (OECD, 2012, p. 21[7]). Common terminology can help members identify which among them are working with which CSOs or types of CSOs – important information to help members choose relevant CSOs to partner with. It also fosters greater transparency and comparability across members' work with CSOs.

Insights from the literature: Ongoing challenges and lessons

Civil society is often characterised as one of three spheres of action, along with government and the private sector. It has been defined as a "sphere of uncoerced human association" within which individuals implement collective action to address shared needs, ideas and interests that they have identified in common (Edwards, 2011, p. 4[8]). CSOs are a formal manifestation of civil society. Civil society is thus considered to be the collection of CSOs and other semi- or non-formal forms of people associating or of associations, as well as the sphere or space in which these interact with each other and with others (Kohler-Koch and Quittkat, 2009[9]). Reference is also made to the civil society or CSO sector, just as government is referred to as the public sector and business as the private sector.[5]

That said, attempts to define or classify civil society and CSOs have been referred to as akin to "nailing jelly to the wall" (Edwards, 2009, p. 4[10]). Given the diversity of association and organising types within the civil society sector, their sometimes informal and fluid nature, and the growth of hybrid types of associations, defining the sector is not always straightforward.[6]

It is evident from the OECD definition of CSOs (Box 1.1) that they are diverse. In the years since publication of this definition, the range of associational types considered to be CSOs appears to even be expanding. For example, some consider social enterprises, a newer organisational form, to be CSOs even though they are a hybrid form of non-profit and for-profit organisations (Smith, 2010[11]). These provide goods and services in the market but, like more traditional CSO forms, they have some form of social impact as their primary objective (OECD/European Union, 2017, p. 22[12]). Foundations and the growing and varied forms of philanthropic initiatives, particularly at decentralised levels, are an organisational type that might be considered in the CSO category.[7]

Box 1.1. OECD definition of CSOs

The OECD defines CSOs as "non-market and non-state organisations outside of the family in which people organise themselves to pursue shared interests in the public domain. They cover a wide range of organisations that include membership-based CSOs, cause-based CSOs and service-oriented CSOs. Examples include community-based organisations and village associations, environmental groups, women's rights groups, farmers' associations, faith-based organisations, labour unions, co-operatives, professional associations, chambers of commerce, independent research institutes, and the not-for-profit media" (OECD, 2010, p. 26[5]).

The DAC reporting directives issued to members refer to non-governmental organisations (NGOs), not CSOs (Box 1.2). However, the definition of an NGO used in these directives closely resembles the OECD (2010[5]) definition of a CSO (Box 1.1). In recent years, DAC publications use CSO, the more current term.[8] This study uses the terms CSO and civil society. The term NGO is occasionally used when a member or other source that uses it is cited in the text.

Box 1.2. DAC definition of an NGO

The DAC defines an NGO as "any non-profit entity in which people organise themselves on a local, national or international level to pursue shared objectives and ideals, without significant government-controlled participation or representation. NGOs include foundations, co-operative societies, trade unions, and ad-hoc entities set up to collect funds for a specific purpose. NGO umbrella organisations and NGO networks are also included" (OECD DAC, 2018, pp. 47-48[13]).

For reporting purposes, the DAC distinguishes NGOs by geographic location and specifically as either international (including NGOs that may have a regional rather than international scope), member country-based, or partner country- or developing country-based NGOs (Box 1.3).[9]

Box 1.3. DAC definitions of NGOs by geographic location

Donor country-based NGO: An NGO that is organised at the national level and based and operated either in the donor country or in another developed country, i.e. one that is not eligible to receive official development assistance (ODA).

International NGO: An NGO that is organised on an international level – meaning either an international co-ordinating body facilitates the work of the NGO members on the international level or the NGO has an extensive network of country or regional offices in the field – and has internationally diversified sources of revenue.

Developing country-based NGO: An NGO that is organised at the national level and based and operated in a developing (ODA-eligible) country.

Source: (OECD DAC, 2018, p. 57[13]), *Converged Statistical Reporting Directives for the Creditor Reporting System (CRS) and the Annual DAC Questionnaire.*

Typically, though not exclusively, member country-based CSOs and international CSOs work in relationships of some form with partner country-based CSOs. These relationships may be ones of mutual support, knowledge exchange and solidarity or they may be more formal partnerships in which the member country-based or international CSO partner plays the role of intermediary in channelling aid. As such, member country-based CSOs and international CSOs can themselves be donors (OECD, 2010, p. 28[5]).[10]

In sum, CSOs comprise a diverse civil society sector, as evidenced by the various types, sizes, locations, mandates, approaches and governance structures seen in the millions of CSOs and non-formal civil society actors across the globe that represent and work with diverse groups of people. The OECD and DAC definitions of NGOs provide a good starting point towards greater commonality of terminology among members and within the OECD.

1.3. Member CSO and/or civil society policies

Existing guidance

Partnering with Civil Society advises members to have in place a civil society or CSO policy, developed and monitored in consultation with CSOs (lesson 1) (OECD, 2012, p. 9[7]). The GPEDC monitoring framework also considers a comprehensive CSO policy document to be a key component of effectiveness for members' work with CSOs (GPEDC, 2018, pp. 14-15[14]). Such a policy document does not need to be a policy per se. It can be a strategy, principles or guidance, for example. What is important is to have a transparent and evidence-based overarching framework for the member's work with CSOs and civil society. The policy document should lay out the member's understanding of civil society and its contribution to development. To guide planning, implementation and evaluation of the member's work with CSOs, the document should further articulate the member's objectives for working with CSOs and civil society and methods of working to meet these objectives.

The existence of a CSO or civil society policy is increasingly evaluated through DAC peer reviews. The 2019-20 *Peer Review Reference Guide* emphasises that members' policy frameworks now should provide sufficient guidance for decision making on channels and engagements with CSOs. Its inclusive development partnerships component specifies that members are expected to articulate a vision of the roles of different actors, including CSOs; support enabling environments and space for civil society; and engage with CSOs at strategic and operational levels (OECD DAC, 2019, p. 11[15]).

Insights from the literature: Ongoing challenges and lessons

Evidence from recent peer reviews suggests that members are adopting CSO policies or policy-like documents. However, there is room for more members to articulate clear visions and normative frameworks for their work with civil society (OECD, 2019[16]).

For example, the 2016 DAC peer review of the Czech Republic called on the country to adopt a vision and policy for its partnerships with civil society and to develop an appropriate mix of funding mechanisms to meet the vision (OECD, 2019, p. 3[16]). Similarly, an independent evaluation of Australia's NGO Cooperation Program in 2015 concluded that greater clarity and common understanding of the programme's objectives, alongside a "complete and internally consistent policy framework", were needed to prevent day-to-day decision making from undermining the programme's principles (Department of Foreign Affairs and Trade of Australia and Coffey International Development, 2015[17]) . This conclusion provided motivation for the development of Australia's 2015 framework document, *DFAT and NGOs: Effective Development Partners* (Department of Foreign Affairs and Trade of Australia, 2015[18]). In another example, the Swiss Agency for Development and Cooperation (SDC) developed its 2019 policy-like document, *SDC Guidance for Engagement with CSOs*, based in part on a 2017 evaluation recommendation to clarify the purpose, objectives, target group and modus operandi of its institutional partnerships with CSOs (Swiss Agency for Development and Cooperation, 2019[19]; IOD PARC, 2017, p. 47[20]).

There is growing recognition of the need for whole-of-government policy coherence on civil society-related issues in addition to CSO policies. This is not addressed in *Partnering with Civil Society*. The importance of integrating civil society considerations, including civic space analysis, across a range of policy realms is gaining attention, especially given the trend of restrictions on civil space and in an environment where member interests are increasingly focused on private sector development, trade and security (Wood, 2019, pp. 414-415, 448-449[21]; Molenaers, Faust and Dellepiane, 2015[22]). These considerations encompass not only development, but also foreign policy and diplomacy and policies on trade and business, security, and technology.[11] Overall, momentum is building to work towards consistency of vision in relation to CSOs' roles and value added and to be explicit about and address competing priorities (CONCORD Sweden, 2018, p. 5[23]; Civil Society Summit, 2019, pp. 6-7[24]; International Center for Not-for-Profit Law, 2018, p. 21[25]).

In sum, absent a policy, members risk that their work with CSOs is ad hoc or guided only by the existence of a CSO budget line, rather than being strategically designed to meet development objectives. A policy can help members to better pursue coherence between objectives and their methods of working with CSOs and civil society. The existence of an up-to-date policy developed in collaboration with civil society helps to ensure the relevance of members' aims and work with the sector. By providing a transparent framework, a policy is a source of common understanding of why and how a member works with CSOs, and it is a source of trust with CSOs. Members' policy visions, as well as policy coherence, can be reinforced through integration of civil society-related issues in broader development co-operation policies and in other policy realms.

1.4. Objectives for working with CSOs and civil society

Existing guidance

Partnering with Civil Society recommends that members clearly articulate in their policies the objective or objectives for working with CSOs and civil society (lesson 1). The guidance effectively addresses two types of objectives in particular. The first type of objective for working with CSOs and civil society is to strengthen a pluralist (i.e. diverse) and independent civil society in partner countries (lesson 2). The second type of objective for working with CSOs and civil society is to help achieve other development objectives besides strengthening civil society in partner countries (lessons 3 and 4) (OECD, 2012, pp. 9, 13, 17, 21[7]).

To help understand the distinction between these two types of objectives, it is useful to consider CSOs and civil society as having both "intrinsic and instrumental value" (UN, 2017, p. 4[26]). Intrinsic value means a strong, pluralist and independent civil society is an asset in and of itself, just as a strong public sector or private sector are valuable assets. Thus, strengthening civil society is an objective worth supporting in its own right (OECD, 2010, pp. 29, 106[5]). Instrumental value centres on CSOs as an instrument – i.e. a means to deliver various other development objectives.

The first type of objective recognises that a strong civil society is an essential prerequisite for any country's social, economic and democratic development. Notably, this first objective flows from statements and commitments made in the context of the aid and development effectiveness agenda. The 2011 Busan Partnership Agreement, for example, commits adherents to enabling CSOs to exercise their roles as independent development actors in their own right, as does paragraph 11c of the more recent 2016 GPEDC Nairobi Outcome Document (OECD, 2011[3]; GPEDC, 2016[27]). As independent development actors in their own right, CSOs are recognised as having their own priorities and plans and approaches to achieving such priorities. The legitimacy of CSOs as independent actors is derived from varied sources: from their constituents, which may be CSO members or groups or individuals that they serve or represent; from their governance and accountability systems; from their expertise and experience; from the development results they achieve; and from the civic values that guide them (OECD, 2010, p. 27[5]; Van

Rooy, 2004[28]).[12] The ability of CSOs to operate as independent development actors is also embedded in international law, particularly in the right to freedom of association and the principles that flow from it (World Movement for Democracy Secretariat and International Center for Not-for-Profit Law, 2012[29]).

Partnering with Civil Society calls on members to promote enabling environments for CSOs in partner countries, understood as the "political, financial, legal and policy context" affecting how CSOs carry out their work (lesson 2) (OECD, 2012, p. 13[7]). In recognition of the aid and development effectiveness commitments to promote enabling environments for civil society, the GPEDC monitors and reports on member practice in this regard, most recently in its 2019 progress report (OECD/UNDP, 2019[30]).[13]

The second type of objective recognises that CSOs are important partners in implementing members' programmes in specific sectors or themes (e.g. health, education, democratisation and gender equality) and in raising public awareness about development in member countries.[14] The second type of objective sees CSOs as implementers on behalf of members. As such, they are channels for members' financial support, acting as intermediaries between members, other CSOs, communities and beneficiaries to implement programmes with specific objectives and often objectives defined by the member (OECD, 2010, p. 28[5]).

The second type of objective for working with civil society recognises the important role that civil society can and does play in humanitarian relief. In 2019, members adopted the DAC Recommendation on the Humanitarian-Development-Peace Nexus, which applies across members' work with civil society and the full spectrum of humanitarian, development and peace actors (OECD DAC, 2019[31]). The Recommendation requires members to strengthen policy and operational coherence between humanitarian, development and peace efforts, with the "aim of effectively reducing people's needs, risks and vulnerabilities, supporting prevention efforts and thus, shifting from delivering humanitarian assistance to ending need" (OECD DAC, 2019[31]). An important aspect of this involves members strengthening their engagement with CSOs across the nexus; ensuring that civil society has the space, resources and capacity to contribute; and drawing on CSOs' proximity to vulnerable populations and their capacity to advocate for and on behalf of vulnerable groups.

Insights from the literature: Ongoing challenges and lessons

Once members set out their objectives for working with CSOs and civil society, they need to consider what methods of working with civil society are best suited to meet these objectives. Little in the literature covers members' objectives for working with CSOs and civil society per se. Rather, there is coverage of members' financial support mechanisms and other working methods. The remaining sections of this chapter focus largely on the literature pertaining to such mechanisms and methods.

Insights are available on members' efforts to strengthen civil society in partner countries by promoting enabling environments in those countries. A key finding of the GPEDC 2019 progress report is that in 57% of countries, CSOs reported that development partners "only occasionally include elements of an enabling environment for CSOs in their policy dialogue with partner country governments" (OECD/UNDP, 2019, p. 132[30]). Development partners, however, assess themselves as more frequently promoting enabling environments in policy dialogue with partner country governments, reporting that they do so only occasionally in 30% of countries but more systematically in 40% of countries (OECD/UNDP, 2019, p. 133[11]).

This discrepancy may be attributable to the fact that sometimes members engage in dialogue with partner country governments on issues around the enabling environment using quiet, non-public dialogue and diplomacy tactics of which CSOs would not necessarily be aware. At other times, members may go so far as to condition their government-to-government support on partner country governments' commitments and actions to provide an enabling environment for civil society. Dialogue, quiet or otherwise, is done bilaterally or collaboratively with other members or through multilateral bodies. The Community of

Democracies Working Group on Enabling and Protecting Civil Society is one example of collective action in this regard. Comprised of members (and CSOs), the Working Group monitors and disseminates information on the environment for civil society worldwide, encourages its participants to take diplomatic steps when threats arise, and raises awareness about the issue (Community of Democracies, 2016[32]). The Open Government Partnership (OGP), which regards space for civil society (i.e. civic space) as "the fundamental underpinning for open government" that its members must include in their action plans, is another example of collective action to promote enabling environments for civil society (Open Government Partnership, 2019, p. 6[33]). The OGP monitors implementation of its members' action plans so that performance may be improved through dialogue and peer pressure.

The International Centre for Not-for-Profit Law (2018, p. 4[25]), in *Effective Donor Responses to the Challenge of Closing Civic Space*, suggests that to defend and promote enabling environments, members complement their own dialogue with partner country governments by encouraging dialogue between government, parliaments and civil society as a means of building mutual understanding and potentially countering the mistrust that can fuel partner country governments' disenabling tactics. They can also assist partner country governments in building more enabling environments for civil society, for instance through support to institutions such human rights commissions and bodies responsible for civil society regulation.

Other recent publications detail additional strategies members can pursue to strengthen civil society in partner countries through the promotion of enabling environments. European Funders for Social Change, the Human Rights Funders Network and the European Foundation Centre recommend, among other things, identifying and working with private sector allies to promote civic space, including in the private sector's own practices in partner countries (Ariadne, International Human Rights Funders Group and European Foundation Centre, 2015, pp. 10-11[34]). The B Team has outlined the "business case" for protection and promotion of enabling environments for civil society, linking civic freedoms data to countries' economic performance (Hogg and Hodess, 2018[35]). An OECD policy paper sets out possible actions to address the deleterious impacts of digital transformation on civic space, such as strengthening the international regulation of corporate governance of digital service providers so they are more accountable and responsive to the adverse effects that their products, services and business operations have on users' rights (OECD, 2020[36]).

As the 2019 DAC Recommendation on the Humanitarian-Development-Peace Nexus is rolled out and its implementation monitored, evidence and lessons will become available regarding whether and how members are reflecting the nexus in their objectives for working with civil society.[15]

In sum, members should clearly articulate their objective or objectives for working with CSOs and civil society. One important type of objective is to strengthen a pluralist and independent civil society in partner countries, recognising the intrinsic value of an independent and pluralist civil society for a nation's social, economic and democratic development. A second type of objective for working with CSOs and civil society is to meet other development objectives besides that of strengthening civil society, recognising the instrumental value of CSOs as partners in implementing members' programmes in specific sectors or themes (e.g. health, education, democratisation and gender). Once there is clarity of objectives, methods of working with CSOs can be better designed to meet them.

Where members seek to pursue the objective of strengthening civil society, myriad strategies are available – apart from but complementary to their CSO support – that can be investigated and implemented. Dialogue with partner country governments on enabling environment issues is one such strategy that needs attention. Complementary strategies include promoting dialogue between CSOs and governments, participating in multilateral bodies, investing in partner country government institutions and capacities, and engaging with private sector allies.

When articulating their objectives and the methods to be used to meet the objectives, members should also bear in mind the 2019 DAC Recommendation on the Humanitarian-Development-Peace Nexus.

Otherwise, the need for humanitarian assistance will continue unabated as the underlying causes of humanitarian crises are not addressed.

1.5. How financial support is provided

Existing guidance

Partnering with Civil Society identifies action points addressing members' mechanisms of financial support for CSOs. First, it proposes that members maintain a mix of financial support mechanisms for CSOs (lesson 7). Having a mix of mechanisms in place helps to make funding available to a range of CSO types and can help members to meet a range of objectives in different contexts. Second, the report also stipulates that members' funding mechanisms should match their stated purpose or objectives for working with CSOs (lesson 7). Third, and relatedly, it states that members should find a balance in their CSO funding mechanisms between the conditions they attach to funding, on one hand, and respect for the role of CSOs as independent development actors with their own mandates and objectives, on the other (lesson 6) (OECD, 2012, pp. 27, 31[7]).

As discussed in Section 1.4, members' funding mechanisms can be designed to meet two types of objectives; these are relevant to lessons 6 and 7. One objective is to strengthen a pluralist (i.e. diverse) and independent civil society in partner countries. The other is to achieve an array of additional, unrelated development objectives (e.g. in health, education, humanitarian assistance, etc.). The funding mechanism most often used to strengthen civil society as an objective in its own right is core support (also referred to as institutional, budget, strategic, unrestricted or unearmarked support). This mechanism comprises support to CSOs "with respect for their independence and right of initiative"; in other words, core support is provided for CSOs to pursue their own missions, objectives, priorities and approaches (Sida, 2019, p. 11[37]). Financial support mechanisms to meet other development objectives are most often provided in the form of project or programme support, wherein CSOs are supported as implementing agents or instruments on behalf of the member. This support tends to come with conditions attached.

Insights from the literature: Ongoing challenges and lessons

In DAC terms, the distinction between support *to* CSOs and support *through* CSOs (Box 1.4) is the most readily available source of information to assess members' support for these two broad objectives (strengthening civil society and meeting other member-defined objectives) and, relatedly, the degree to which such support is for CSOs as independent development actors or comes with member conditions. Support *to* CSOs is core support and, as noted, is most conducive to meeting an objective of strengthening an independent and pluralist civil society in partner countries (OECD, 2012, p. 14[7]). In contrast, support flows *through* CSOs when CSOs operate on behalf of the member as implementers of projects or programmes with specific member-defined objectives.

Statistics from the OECD on members' flows *to* and *through* CSOs between 2010 and 2017 show a high level of flows *through* CSOs relative to flows *to* CSOs (Figure 2.5 and Tables B.1 and B.2 in Annex B). This difference suggests that member funding mechanisms are mostly geared to meet objectives other than that of strengthening civil society and come with conditions rather than respecting the role of CSOs as independent actors.

Box 1.4. Reporting aid *to* and *through* NGOs/CSOs*

Aid to NGOs covers official funds paid over to non-governmental organisations for use at the latter's discretion. Aid *through* NGOs covers official funds made available to NGOs for use on behalf of the official sector, in connection with purposes designated by the official sector, or known to and approved by the official sector.

Aid to NGOs means official contributions to programmes and activities which NGOs have developed themselves, and which they implement on their own authority and responsibility. *Aid through NGOs* means payments by the official sector for NGOs to implement projects and programmes which the official sector has developed, and for which it is ultimately responsible. The latter includes "joint financing" schemes where government agencies and NGOs consult about activities, jointly approve them and/or share their funding.

* The DAC reporting directives use the term NGOs and also apply in this study to CSOs.

Source: (OECD DAC, 2018, p. 58[13]), Converged Statistical Reporting Directives for the Creditor Reporting System (CRS) and the Annual DAC Questionnaire.

That said, OECD statistics on flows *to* and *through* CSOs do not reliably capture the volume of flows for one or the other of the two objectives. Members' *through* support may overlap or straddle different objectives along a spectrum. That is, members' CSO funding either is responsive to and aligns with CSOs' priorities as independent development actors to different degrees or, on the contrary, this funding is conditional (or earmarked) and thus directs or steers CSOs to the member's priorities. The spectrum of directiveness of non-core support is referred to in the multilateral system as involving tightly or strictly earmarked non-core funding or softly earmarked non-core funding (OECD DAC, 2019[38]).

As an illustration of this spectrum, a member may design a project support mechanism via a call for proposals (*through* support) that is focused on a high-level, member-defined objective. If the mechanism is responsive to CSO submissions in line with the CSO's self-defined priorities, the funding could be considered as softly earmarked. The projects and programme support of the Austrian Development Agency (ADA) *through* CSOs is one example. ADA co-funds projects and programmes that are initiated by CSOs but match Austria's high-level goals (Ceelen, Wood and Huesken, 2019[39]) Another example is where a *through* funding mechanism may be used to support a CSO acting as intermediary between the member and CSOs in partner countries. The objective of the support, however, may be to strengthen the end recipient CSOs and civil society more broadly in partner countries. This is the case with Swedish CSOs that are the member's framework partners and receive what is reported as *through* support while in turn, in some instances, channelling some of the funds they receive to CSOs in partner countries as *to* support (core funding).

These examples suggest that the ratio of members' *to* and *through* financial support does not provide sufficient information to determine whether members' support mechanisms match objectives or assess the balance between their support for CSOs with conditions attached and support to CSOs as independent development actors. The literature on the experience of CSOs with both *to* and *through* support, and on the advantages and disadvantages of each, helps to complement the information that can be gleaned from the data.

A number of literature sources reinforce the prevalence of *through* support that is conditional or earmarked to meet member-defined objectives. The GPEDC 2019 monitoring exercise finds CSOs in 82% of monitored countries reported that the funding priorities and mechanisms of support for CSOs are "driven by development partners' own programming interests or tied directly to implementation of their own priorities", such that CSOs "consider themselves more as implementers rather than as equal partners and actors in their own right" (OECD/UNDP, 2019, p. 133[11]).[16] This conforms to findings elsewhere that members' support *through* CSOs is experienced as being strongly "donor-driven" (i.e. conditional, directive or earmarked) and designed to meet members' pre-defined objectives (Bushan et al., 2018, p. 162[21]). Some member evaluations attest to the conditional nature of financial support for CSOs while highlighting the pitfalls. For example, an evaluation of civil society support modalities at the Swedish International Development Cooperation Agency (Sida) headquarters and Swedish embassies over 2007-13 found that CSOs were mainly used as a means or a tool to implement programming targeting objectives set by Sida and the embassies (Nilsson et al., 2013, pp. 79, 84, 88[40]). The evaluation further noted that rather than strengthening civil society, this instrumental approach "undermine[s] the credibility of CSOs, weakens their accountability to their own stakeholders and shift[s] this towards the donors, make[s] it difficult for CSO [sic] to engage in longer term planning such as for their own policy and capacity development, and make[s] the claims by adversaries that certain CSOs are donor agents more believable among the public" (Nilsson et al., 2013, p. 90[40]) This approach can lead CSOs to deviate from their mandates and strategic plans as they seek to match donors' ever-changing priorities (Sida, 2019, p. 10[37]).

A joint evaluation of member support for civil society engagement in policy dialogue, led by the Danish International Development Agency (Danida), reached a similar conclusion. It found that when members' own agendas dominate the CSO support they provide, civil society's independence and initiatives are threatened and the concept of a vibrant and pluralist civil society as a public good or "an end in itself" is undermined (Itad Ltd and COWI, 2012, p. 101[41]).[17] Given changing member priorities, this also threatens investment in long-term change processes and can lead to the neglect of some agendas that are worthy of support because they may not fall within member priorities of the moment (Itad Ltd and COWI, 2012, p. 101[41]).

Funding mechanisms designed to meet "donor-defined" objectives also tend to be for short-term initiatives, with what has been called a growing "projectisation" of members' CSO support (CIVICUS, 2015, pp. 150-151[42]). On one hand, short-term project support is appreciated by small or more nascent CSOs as it tends to have lower barriers to entry and is thus easier to access than core support. On the other hand, its short-term, directive nature means it lacks predictability, so that CSOs struggle to implement the actions necessary for long-term change (results) and to build and maintain their fundamental capacities, expertise and operations (CIVICUS, 2015, pp. 150-152[42]; Haynes, Ireland and Duke, 2019, p. 4[43]). Further, as CSOs "hop from subject to subject" in search of support for one short-term project after another, they are less able to build and maintain the relationships with constituencies and beneficiaries that are a necessary component of local ownership and CSOs' accountability (CIVICUS, 2015, p. 152[42]). A recent study on funding of CSOs and their networks concludes there is a "disconnect between managerialist approaches to civil society funding, characterised by competitive, short-termist and results-driven agendas, and the desire of institutional donors to support a sustainable and thriving civil society through flexible and responsive funding" (Haynes, Ireland and Duke, 2019, p. 4[43]).

These issues are further illustrated in members' efforts to strengthen the coherence of humanitarian, development and peace actions. As noted in a 2017 evaluation of Finnish CSOs, the bifurcation of humanitarian and development financing mechanisms can limit the ability of CSOs to operate in the humanitarian-development nexus, given the separate windows and time frames of members' funding, an absence of flexibility to frame programming around the nexus, and the short duration of humanitarian funding cycles (Brusset et al., 2017, pp. 3, 15, 19[44]). CSOs' own siloed operating modalities and limited long-term consideration of exit strategies in humanitarian programming are a related impediment that, combined with member conditions, results in compartmentalisation rather than the co-ordination and coherence needed to address the nexus (Brusset et al., 2017, pp. 15, 16[44]).

Core funding *to* CSOs averts some of the reported disadvantages of donor-driven, projectised support *through* CSOs. Core funding tends to be relatively long term (five years or more) and thus somewhat predictable, while it is also considered relatively flexible in that it supports a CSO's mission or objectives rather than a specific project (Wood and Fällman, 2013, p. 147[45]; National Audit Office, 2006, pp. 18-19[46]). Predictability and flexibility are said to enable CSOs to implement the kinds of actions needed for long-term transformative change, address new issues and opportunities arising in changing contexts and innovate, and help to foster collaboration and learning across CSOs (Itad Ltd and COWI, 2012[41]; Sida, 2019[37]). Moreover, support of CSOs' own objectives allows them to pursue their work in ways that are locally owned and demand-driven rather than donor-driven. Core funding enables CSOs to focus on implementation of their core work of achieving development results and on their relationships with partner country constituencies. It also means more time and resources are available for CSOs to maintain their day-to-day operations while investing in strengthening their organisational capacities (Staniforth, 2009, p. 9[47]).

Core funding has challenges, however. Members fear that recipient CSOs may become overly reliant on such funding and lose motivation to innovate (Staniforth, 2009, p. 8[47]). The most significant challenge is demonstrating results. Unless objectives for the core funding agreement and associated results and indicators are clearly articulated, CSOs and members that provide core support can find it difficult to demonstrate the effectiveness of core funding (National Audit Office, 2006, pp. 18-19[46]; Staniforth, 2009, pp. 8-9[47]).[18] Pressure to demonstrate results was one of the reasons that the Department for International Development (DFID) of the United Kingdom switched from core-type support for CSOs, under what were called Partnership Programme Agreements, to project support using calls for proposals following its 2016 *Civil Society Partnerships Review*. Its aim, in part, was to be able to better assess CSO proposals on value for money – that is, on development results achieved for money spent (DFID, 2016, p. 11[48]). OECD DAC recommends that members make better use of the recipient's results monitoring and reporting systems to help resolve the challenge around demonstrating results, although this requires acknowledging that results might not be fully attributable to the member's contribution (OECD DAC, 2019, p. 6[38]).

Processes using competitive calls for proposals have been found to have a mixed record as a means of allocating funding *through* CSOs.[19] On one hand, calls for proposals are appreciated for their transparency, as the requirements are open for all to see (Karlstedt et al., 2015, p. 22[49]). On the other hand, calls tend to be donor-driven, given that parameters (conditions) for the competition must be set by the member. In addition, competitive processes "can inhibit or distort co-operation between CSOs operating in the same space for the same goals of leaving no one behind" (Bushan et al., 2018, p. 163[6]). Calls are also found to place a high administrative burden on both members and CSOs due to the need to process many applicants, of which only some are successful (Karlstedt et al., 2015, p. 22[49]). A 2012 evaluation of CSO support provided by Australian Aid (then called AusAID) noted the further challenge that smaller, more nascent CSOs often lack the time, resources and capacity to fulfil the demands of competitive calls and so do not bother to apply, limiting outreach (Howell and Hall, 2012, p. 20[50]).

Notably, core funding shares these challenges of administrative burden and accessibility. There are significant administrative costs in initially identifying appropriate CSOs, taking due diligence steps to screen for systems and other capacity, negotiating terms and outcomes, and building trust (Itad Ltd and COWI, 2012, p. 88[41]; Karlstedt et al., 2015, p. 22[49]). These are front-end obstacles and costs, however. Over the long term, core support should come with reduced transaction costs as these long-term arrangements with trusted partners require less frequent and more strategic reporting than project/programme support requires (Itad Ltd and COWI, 2012, p. 88[41]).

Moreover, smaller and less experienced CSOs tend to have difficulty meeting the criteria for programme and financial management capacity and track record and as a result, they cannot access core support (Ceelen, Wood and Huesken, 2019, p. 38[39]). Another of the aims of DFID's switch from core-type support to project support following the *Civil Society Partnerships Review* was to make funding available for a broader range of CSOs, including smaller ones that had struggled to meet the Partnership Programme Agreement funding requirements (DFID, 2016, p. 9[48]). Core support mechanisms can be designed to be accessible to smaller and less experienced CSOs, however. Sida, for instance, is actively exploring fresh approaches to core support for smaller CSOs and diverse civil society actors, including by experimenting with a guarantee instrument to enable financial risk sharing between Sida and its Swedish CSO partners (Sida, 2019, pp. 12, 13[37]).

In sum, the ratio of members' *to* and *through* financial support for CSOs is too blunt an instrument for assessing the degree to which members' financial support is designed to meet the strengthening civil society objective or, in contrast, to meet other, member-defined objectives. Nuanced interpretation is required to better understand the degree to which a member's t*hrough* funding mechanism is more or less conditional and directive.

There is room for both types of financial support mechanisms for CSOs, as each has different advantages and disadvantages. When designing mechanisms and determining the appropriate mechanism mix, members should keep in mind the objective of strengthening a pluralist civil society in partner countries. Ideally, members would have mechanisms that aim to meet this objective. At minimum, they need to ensure that their financial support for CSOs does no harm to CSOs and the civil society sector.

The risk of harm relates to the fact that a reliance on financial support mechanisms *through* CSOs, and in which objectives are defined by members alone, can undercut CSOs' ability to operate in ways that are demand-driven and responsive to the priorities of the CSOs' partners and constituents on the ground, thus hindering local ownership and accountability. Significantly, this in turn can fuel perceptions that CSOs are simply agents of foreign powers – that is, of members. Additionally, reliance on *through* support can make it difficult for CSOs to plan for the long term and respond flexibly to changing contexts. It can hinder CSOs' investment in their institutional capacity. Further, such reliance can lead to gaps in support for civil society actors in partner countries. When these actors are not aligned with member-defined priorities, members may invest in and indeed foster civil society and CSOs that are not sufficiently locally rooted and accountable and do not reflect the real range of civil society actors in partner countries.

On the whole, therefore, working with CSOs solely as a means to reach other, member-defined objectives not only fails to meet the objective of strengthening a pluralist civil society in partner countries. It can undermine this objective. Core support for CSOs can address some of the issues arising from donor-driven *through* support. However, core support also has potential downsides that need to be mitigated, among them the due diligence standards that can make core support less available to a wide swathe of civil society.

1.6. Who receives financial support

Existing guidance

The 2012 *Partnering with Civil Society* guidance does not state outright that there is a need for more direct financing for partner country CSOs. However, this is implied in the call to expand the scope of members' CSO partnerships to better meet objectives, including the objective of strengthening civil society in partner countries (lessons 4 and 7) (OECD, 2012, pp. 21, 31[7]). The need for more direct CSO financing also flows logically from the development effectiveness commitment to local ownership; providing more support and funding tools for local organisations is also a Grand Bargain commitment (workstream 2) (Inter-Agency Standing Committee, 2020[51]).[20]

Noting the tendency of members to support CSOs they are most familiar with – that is, well-established, international development or rights and democracy CSOs – the guidance also encourages outreach to a broader swathe of civil society (lesson 4) (OECD, 2012, p. 4[7]). Support for and engagement with diverse civil society actors can help members to work with the most appropriate types of actors (formal or otherwise) to reach a given objective in a given context.

Insights from the literature: Ongoing challenges and lessons

Members' financial support is largely for member country-based or international CSOs, according to OECD statistics. In 2017, member country CSOs received approximately ten times more member funding than did partner country CSOs. Statistics on flows for different types of CSOs are presented in Figure 2.8 in Chapter 2. Studies show that even where partner country-based CSOs have adopted the professionalised, managerialist practices that help them to meet member requirements (e.g. use of monitoring and evaluation systems), members still tend to prefer to support non-local CSOs (Suarez and Gugerty, 2016, p. 2634[52]).

As noted, member country and international CSOs, for the most part, work with partner country CSOs (or other organisational types) at partner country level, which often involves a capacity development component. In effect, these partner country-based CSOs end up facing challenges like those discussed in Section 1.5 in terms of the necessity to meet member-defined priorities, as these cascade down via member country or international CSOs (OECD/UNDP, 2016, p. 47[53]). Member country and international CSOs have some work to do to change their ways of doing business towards "role sharing and the strengthening of local structures" (Bushan et al., 2018, p. 164[6]). As they also explore how to provide more financial support directly to partner country CSOs, members can ensure that their financial support mechanisms better enable member country and international CSOs to make such changes by addressing some of the challenges discussed in Section 1.5.

Even capacity development efforts by member country or international CSOs produce mixed results for partner country CSOs. Brusset et al. (2017, p. 14[44]), in their evaluation of CSOs receiving programme-based and humanitarian assistance support from Finland, found the relationships of Finnish CSOs with their partner CSOs "are often directive rather than aiming at greater independence of local civil society, as relations with local partners are more sub-contracting than consultative". As a result, capacity development of partner country CSOs is focused on effective project implementation rather than on organisational capacity development or on building accountability at partner country level through constituency feedback mechanisms or other means (Brusset et al., 2017, pp. 45-46[44]). Similarly, a 2018 evaluation of Norway's CSO support found that Norwegian CSOs' capacity development of partner country CSOs has focused more on administration, finance and programme implementation and less on the partners' internal governance or accountability systems (Tjønneland et al., 2018, p. 50[54]). A 2018 evaluation of Icelandic CSOs also concluded that some CSO projects had not invested in organisational capacity development of local partners and, on the whole, had "done little to strengthen the partner CSOs at country level" (Ljungman and Nilsson, 2018, p. 10[55]).

As discussed, members' CSO funding tends to favour better known, formal CSOs, which means that members' support may overlook the varied types of civil society actors, such as traditional forms (e.g. faith-based, trade unions, professional associations, etc.); the growing body of hybrid forms including social enterprises; and other more informal, fluid forms of civil society action that are on the rise (Youngs, 2015[56]). While the CSOs that members are most used to working with may have "high visibility", they may be marginally significant relative to the "wider array of associational life" active in partner countries (Sogge, 2019[57]).

Member evaluations, noting that broadening the reach of their support is a challenge for members, make similar recommendations to those in *Partnering with Civil Society* (OECD, 2012, p. 21[7]). An evaluation of Swedish support, for instance, noted a tendency to favour "large, well-reputed CSOs that can handle large amounts of resources" that is due in part to a shortage of member resources to administer CSO support (Nilsson et al., 2013, p. 88[40]). Members are being urged to identify ways to support informal, sometimes temporary civil society actors, actions and processes (Itad Ltd and COWI, 2012, pp. 101, 110-111[41]) that occasionally "bypass formal CSOs" (INTRAC, 2013, p. 7[58]). Innovative thinking is needed to address the new challenge of engaging with these varied actors and actions, but looking "beyond the more 'recognisable' types of civil society groups" that are operating in the development field to sometimes more "enduring institutions that command significant authority and legitimacy in society" can go a long way towards broadening the reach of members' civil society support (Howell and Hall, 2012, pp. 5, 7[50]).

Multi-donor pooled funding has been suggested as one mechanism that can help members increase their direct support for partner country CSOs and potentially broaden members' reach to a greater diversity of civil society actors (INTRAC, 2014, p. 4[59]). For example and despite their modest budgets, some women's funds are able to reach small local women's organisations and movements with limited absorptive capacity. The funds provide modest grants (USD 10 000-30 000) to these civil society actors that members or multilateral donors may be unable to directly support for administrative reasons (Wood and Fällman, 2019, p. 10[60]). Where members are averse to risks that they associate with direct support for partner country CSOs or to less-known civil society actors, pooled funding allows members to share these risks. Further, in partner countries where environments for civil society are less than enabling, multi-donor funds can demonstrate greater solidarity for civil society groups compared to individually funded programmes. If such funds take on an identity separate from the funding sources, this independent image can also help improve the fund's legitimacy.

Nonetheless, there are identified risks with multi-donor pooled funds of unintended consequences, among them displacement of alternative funding opportunities; narrowing of CSO access to interaction with members; their potential for being overly supply-driven, based on member-defined objectives; the crowding out of nascent CSOs; and the possibility such funds may generate competition rather than collaboration among CSOs (INTRAC, 2014, p. 21[59]; CIVICUS, 2015, p. 150[42]). Many of these risks can be mitigated with careful design, ongoing monitoring and member engagement. Specific mitigating strategies are discussed in a *Guidance Note for Danish Missions* developed by the International NGO Training and Research Centre (INTRAC) and Danida (INTRAC and Ministry of Foreign Affairs of Denmark, 2014[61]).

In sum, more support should be provided directly to partner country CSOs and support needs to reach a diversity of civil society actors. Both of these actions are appropriate to strengthening civil society in partner countries. While it is commendable to integrate capacity development of partner country CSOs into CSO support, this should be designed to meet local CSO needs and not only programme implementation and monitoring needs. Multi-donor funds are another option, with potential pitfalls that need to be watched for and avoided.

1.7. Dialogue and consultation with CSOs and civil society

Existing guidance

One of the 12 lessons presented in the 2012 guidance, *Partnering with Civil Society*, calls on members to make their policy dialogue and consultations with CSOs more strategic, useful and meaningful (lesson 5) (OECD, 2012, p. 23[7]). Dialogue is mutually beneficial for CSOs and members. It allows members to tap into the knowledge, expertise and experience of CSOs, which can help to make members' policies and programmes more relevant, responsive and likely to achieve sustainable development results. For CSOs, dialogue provides a channel for information gathering and influencing. For both, it is a way to build mutual trust and accountability and to foster and maintain communication and connections beyond the funding relationship.

Engaging in dialogue with civil society is also integral to SDG 16, which addresses the need for responsive, inclusive, participatory and representative decision making. Moreover, the type of multi-stakeholder partnerships called for in SDG 17 need to be grounded in dialogue inclusive of CSOs. Notably, the 2019 OECD Recommendation of the Council on Open Government calls on OECD members to provide "equal and fair opportunities to be informed and consulted", to engage stakeholders "in all phases of the policy-cycle and service design and delivery", and to make specific efforts to reach out to the most "relevant, vulnerable, underrepresented, or marginalised groups in society" (OECD, 2017[62]). Dialogue is a key transparency tool for members as part of their commitments to open governments.

Insights from the literature: Ongoing challenges and lessons

The GPEDC 2019 progress report concludes that there is room for improvement in members' dialogue and consultation with CSOs on the design, implementation and monitoring of members' development co-operation policies and programmes at partner country level.[21] Though CSOs were consulted in the preparation of 75% of development partners' country strategies, multilateral development banks and United Nations (UN) agencies undertook consultations more often than did members (OECD/UNDP, 2016, p. 129[53]). CSOs in partner countries viewed, consultation with members as not systematic but rather episodic and unpredictable (OECD/UNDP, 2019, p. 130[30]). When dialogue does take place, these CSOs reported, the agendas are set by members rather than being jointly defined and inclusiveness is not achieved (OECD/UNDP, 2019, p. 130[30]). Anecdotal evidence also suggests a lack of co-ordination of dialogue with CSOs at partner country level; this can increase transaction costs of dialogue for CSOs and lead to dialogue fatigue (OECD/UNDP, 2019, p. 130[30]).[22]

Recent studies and evaluations point to gaps in the area of dialogue with CSOs at member country level as well. Abrahamson et al. (2019[63]), researchers for the London-based CSO network Bond, argue that DFID, in its relationships with CSOs, has moved away from an interactive partnership approach and towards a more transactional, contractual approach that is tied to funding agreements. This shift, they note, is partly responsible for blocking full implementation of the 2016 *Civil Society Partnership Review* pledge to increase regular, structured policy dialogue with CSOs (Abrahamson et al., 2019[63]; DFID, 2016, pp. 5, 11[48]).[23] A 2016 evaluation of Finland's programme-based support through CSOs noted that CSOs should have more opportunities for dialogue with the broader Ministry for Foreign Affairs beyond the Ministry's Civil Society Unit; this would enable CSOs to share information on the substantive issues they see in their day-to-day work in partner countries including civic space restrictions, which in turn could help to strengthen coherence in the Finnish response and interventions overall (Stage et al., 2016, pp. 20, 24, 26[64]). A generally positive review of the European Commission (EC) Policy Forum for Development (which takes place in Brussels and at partner country level) identified interest in more in-depth dialogue with greater possibility of actually impacting EC policies, and the need for participant selection criteria to ensure appropriate representativity, among other findings (Garcia, 2016, p. 2[65]).

There are numerous resources and examples of good practice in design and implementation of dialogue and in consultation with CSOs. The OECD DAC (2018[66]) Framework for Dialogue between the DAC and Civil Society Organisations, for instance, institutionalises the DAC's CSO consultations and outlines principles, mechanisms and follow-up steps. Also in 2018, the Office of the United Nations High Commissioner for Human Rights, in its *Guidelines for States on the Effective Implementation of the Right to Participate in Public Affairs*, published a series of practical recommendations for institutionalising participation and ensuring meaningful participation at all stages of decision making (UN, 2018[67]). The Task Team's 2019 *Guidance and Good Practice on CSO Development Effectiveness and Enabling Environment* contains tips on how to make dialogue institutionalised, timely, accessible and inclusive and highlights the need for resourcing and capacity development to support CSO participation (Ceelen, Wood and Huesken, 2019[39]). A further example is a 2019 policy brief, developed by the British Columbia Council for International Cooperation and the Canadian Council for International Co-operation, calling for consultation approaches that reflect the transformative elements of the 2030 Agenda such as human rights, participation and leaving no one behind, all of which can strengthen inclusivity (Wayne-Nixon et al., 2019[68])).

In sum, dialogue and consultation with CSOs are integral to members' commitments to openness and transparency. They also foster better and potentially more coherent development co-operation, foreign policies and programmes by taking advantage of CSOs' knowledge, expertise and experience including on civic space challenges. Member dialogue with CSOs needs concerted attention so that it is systematic, predictable and adequately resourced. Aspects of good practice that require attention include joint agenda setting and a process of participant selection that ensures inclusion of varied civil society actors. Absent attention to good practice in dialogue, member policies and programmes risk losing relevance and credibility and members risk being seen as unaccountable to both CSOs and the people they represent.

1.8. Administrative requirements

Existing guidance

Partnering with Civil Society recommends that members work to minimise the administrative burden on themselves and on CSOs that is created by the sometimes onerous procedures and requirements related to proposals, funding applications, reporting and auditing (lesson 8) (OECD, 2012, p. 35[7]). When CSOs are caught up in meeting the varied requirements of multiple members that provide them support, valuable time and resources are not available for CSOs' core work and achievement of development results. The Grand Bargain also recognises the need to better manage the administrative burden associated with humanitarian funding. As delineated in paragraph 1 of workstream 9, dedicated to harmonising and simplifying reporting requirements, Grand Bargain adherents commit to maintain substantive reporting that is of high quality and also "lean enough to allow for the most efficient use of resources to assist people in need" (Inter-Agency Standing Committee, 2020[69]).

Partnering with Civil Society also urges members to reduce transaction costs, for example by ensuring their procedures are strategic, streamlined and flexible; providing multi-year core or programme-based funding; and adapting requirements to contribution size and risk level. Harmonising requirements across members, including through multi-donor pooled funding, is another strategy. Further, members are encouraged to use CSOs' own formats for proposals and reporting and to accept CSOs' own financial audits, where members have assessed these as adequate. Ideally, requirements would be designed to incorporate responsiveness to the priorities and approaches that CSO applicants have themselves identified with their partners and communities at partner country level. Being responsive to CSOs' priorities and approaches can not only reduce transaction costs but also enhance local ownership (lesson 7) (OECD, 2012, p. 31[7]).

Insights from the literature: Ongoing challenges and lessons

Evidence suggests that both CSOs and members face ongoing heavy administrative burdens associated with funding for CSOs. Findings from a CONCORD survey indicate that while the European Union has taken steps to ease some of its procedures and requirements for funding CSOs, these remain "so complex and so numerous that for most organisations they are simply impenetrable" (CONCORD, 2017, p. 20[70]). A recent evaluation of New Zealand's CSO Partnerships Fund found that the process of concept appraisal and contracting was "resource-heavy and lengthy for some partners" (McGillivray et al., 2018, p. 49[71]). As noted by CIVICUS (2015, pp. 144, 152[42]), there is widespread concern that member funding applications and approval processes can be "lengthy and cumbersome" and that the necessity of complying with demanding administrative and reporting requirements drains CSO energies and resources. A CONCORD Sweden (2018, p. 10[23]) report suggests that especially in sensitive environments where civic space is challenged, members should build in flexibility to the requirements they impose on CSOs (e.g. on-site payments versus bank payments, oral versus written follow-up) to allow CSOs to remain focused on their operations and security.

A 2012 study of Norway's civil society support drew attention to the cascading of transaction costs from the Norwegian Agency for Development Cooperation (Norad) through its Norwegian CSO partners and again through to the partner country-level partners of these Norwegian CSOs (Abuom et al., 2012, pp. 6,

43[72]). European CSOs in the ACT Alliance recently set out to reduce the administrative burden on their counterparts in partner countries by harmonising their own requirements for proposals, reporting and contracts. They found themselves limited by the requirements placed on them by their funders, concluding that "detailed, strict and specific back donor requirements are the main challenge" and "need to be more harmonized" (ACT Alliance, 2019, p. 1[73]).

Members have taken steps towards harmonisation of requirements. Multi-donor pooled funds, for instance, emerged as a response to the aid effectiveness principle of co-ordination and harmonisation among members (OECD, 2010, pp. 111-112[5]). These funds not only can help to expand the reach of members' CSO support. They also are a means to manage administrative costs of CSO support, although they are not always effective in this regard if participating members maintain their own administrative requirements or the fund adopts the requirements of the member with the most rigid requirements (INTRAC, 2014, p. 5[59]; Task Team on CSO Development Effectiveness and Enabling Environment, 2014, p. 17[74]).

Beyond pooling, a Sida-led harmonisation initiative involving approximately 15 members sought to reduce transaction costs and promote methods of member support for CSOs that could enhance ownership (Sida, 2019, p. 23[37]). This initiative involved an extensive research process, consultation with CSOs and frank assessment by members of the degree to which harmonisation was possible. It led in 2013 to a Code of Practice on Donor Harmonisation comprised of the Key Principles for Harmonisation and Alignment, a Guideline for Operationalisation of the Key Principles, and a Tool for Commitment and Accountability (Sida, 2019, p. 26[37]). Though participating members appeared prepared to adhere to the Code, the Code continues to lack an institutional home for follow-up.

In sum, heavy administrative requirements are a burden both for members and for CSOs. For CSOs, the day-to-day demands of meeting members' many and varied requirements mean less time, energy and resources are available to dedicate to their core development work. These requirements are a distraction from the achievement of development results that cascade down to CSOs' partners at partner country level. Streamlining of each member's requirements and aligning these where feasible to CSOs' administrative systems can help to addressing the administrative burden for CSOs and members. Harmonisation of member requirements also needs attention, though multi-donor pooled funds are only a partial solution. Work that has already been done, reflected in the Code of Practice on Donor Harmonisation, needs to be revisited.

1.9. Monitoring for results and learning

Existing guidance

Members are under pressure to demonstrate – to their publics, parliaments and other government departments – that their ODA investments deliver development results. This is an understandable and necessary pressure. It is the ability to demonstrate results that helps to maintain buy-in for members' development assistance, whether through CSOs and otherwise. Further, the necessity of showing progress in achieving the 2030 Agenda and the SDGs is reinvigorating interest in results management (Vähämäki and Verger, 2019, pp. 25-26[75]).

The 2012 *Partnering with Civil Society* guidance underscores the importance of demonstrating the results of members' funding for CSOs. But it calls for results that are realistic, relevant and useful to the CSO recipients of funding and, related to the Section 1.8 discussion of administrative requirements, it also calls for monitoring and reporting methods that are not overly burdensome (lesson 10) (OECD, 2012, p. 39[7]). Setting objectives and indicators jointly with CSOs, or even relying on CSO-defined indicators, can help to ensure this relevance and ownership. *Partnering with Civil Society* also encourages the use of monitoring, reporting and evaluations by members and by CSOs, not solely as a compliance tool but also for lesson learning that then together inform the planning and implementation of initiatives (lesson 12) (OECD, 2012, p. 45[7]).

Insights from the literature: Ongoing challenges and lessons

Much has been written about how an inflexible application of results-based management (RBM) can impede the effectiveness of members' work with CSOs. Not only can this increase transaction costs for CSOs and members. It also can hinder risk taking and innovation and favour quantitative, relatively quick-win results rather than the more complex and sometimes unpredictable institutional and social transformations needed for long-term sustainable change. See, for example, (Wood and Fällman, 2013, p. 149[45]; Itad Ltd and COWI, 2012, pp. 7-8[41]; Vähämäki and Verger, 2019, pp. 5, 22[75]). These types of negative effects are reflected in a recent evaluation of Norad's support for Norwegian CSOs. According to the evaluation, RBM comes with a risk of "crowding out" intangible but possibly transformational results while potentially focusing on results that are less relevant to partner country CSOs and their constituencies and beneficiaries (Tjønneland et al., 2018, p. 55[54]). Elsewhere, rigid application of RBM is seen to risk crowding out more nascent CSOs or diverse civil society actors with limited results management experience (INTRAC, 2013, p. 5[58]). The Norwegian evaluation concluded that the increasing emphasis on delivering and documenting results fosters an instrumental approach by Norwegian CSOs, whereby they use their local CSO partners as programme implementers, rather than an intrinsic partnership approach for strengthening civil society in the long term (Tjønneland et al., 2018, p. 52[54]). According to the CIVICUS *2015 State of Civil Society Report*, new ways of measuring CSOs' contributions to development must be found due to the difficulty of proving results of CSO actions that contribute to structural change over time relative to discrete, measurable deliverables (CIVICUS, 2015, p. 152[42]).

The intended aim of the RBM method has always been to allow for iterative programme planning and implementation, i.e. to generate a process of learning from monitoring and adjusting accordingly throughout the programme cycle. As the Ministry of Foreign Affairs of Finland (2015, p. 8[76]) outlined in its 2015 guidance to support RBM across the country's development co-operation, the use of information from results monitoring for the purposes of learning and improving performance is one of the RBM principles. However, Vähämäki and Verger (2019, p. 26[75])], in a recent OECD working paper on learning from RBM evaluations and reviews, conclude that members rarely use results information to inform decisions and provide programming direction, a conclusion that can presumably be extended to members' CSO programming.[24] The issue is not so much RBM per se, but how it is implemented (Vähämäki and Verger, 2019, p. 29[75]). An OECD DAC Evaluation Insights Working Paper noted that a "mechanistic" interpretation of RBM leads CSOs to use monitoring simply to tally results rather than as a tool for lessons learning to inform planning (INTRAC, 2013, p. 5[58]). Evidence also points to gaps in CSOs' capacity to develop sound theories of change and thus to monitor, and learn from, the impacts of CSOs' programmes (INTRAC, 2013, p. 4[58]).

Attention is increasingly focused on the need for results management approaches that are appropriate to the complexities of development and on the need for relevant, locally owned results. Theories of change are meant to be one such approach. A theory of change is akin to a logical framework analysis. The primary difference is that a theory of change is less linear, showing varied possible pathways to change and providing more analytical information as to why these pathways are anticipated (Bisits Bullen, 2014[77]). Adaptive management is also getting increased consideration as a new approach to results management. Central to this approach are a strong power analysis to inform planning and implementation; flexibility, adaptation and path adjustment based on learning in changing contexts; and a high level of trust between members and their implementing partners (Vähämäki and Verger, 2019, pp. 30, 32-33[75]).

Guidance and lessons learning on adaptive management approaches are available from varied sources including the Thinking and Working Politically Community of Practice and Doing Development Differently, which since 2018 has been associated with a new Global Learning for Adaptive Management initiative.[25]

Lessons from member-funded CSOs seeking to implement adaptive management are also emerging, among them the Oxfam From Poverty to Power blog.[26] A recent open access issue of *The Foundation Review* contains insights on collaborative learning and adaptive management from various foundations' programmes that are applicable to members and the CSOs they support.[27] More generally, INTRAC maintains an online monitoring and evaluation resource, the M&E Universe, where short papers on various monitoring, evaluation and learning-related topics can be found.[28]

In sum, monitoring and evaluation is critically important for both members and CSOs to be able to demonstrate that ODA for CSOs is achieving development results. But when monitoring for results becomes less about assessing how transformative a CSO is and more about its compliance with the terms of an agreement, monitoring for results can have counterproductive effects. Overly rigid use of RBM can undermine the very capabilities members cite as reasons they choose to work with CSOs, such as the ability to innovate and take risks; be flexible and responsive to beneficiaries and constituencies on the ground and to changing contexts; and address complex institutional and social transformations needed for long-term sustainable change. Results management needs to be applied in the iterative, adaptive way it was intended to be used, whereby learning and course correction are integrated throughout. An adaptive management approach, inclusive of co-defined or CSO-defined indicators, has the potential to better assess CSOs' contributions to development that go beyond the kind of discrete, measurable outputs that may not even lead to long-term sustainable results.

As members continue to adjust and improve their results management approaches, drawing from the body of good practice and lessons-sharing resources available, investment in CSOs' capacity will continue to be needed.

1.10. Accountability and transparency of CSOs and members

Existing guidance

Partnering with Civil Society points to the need for increased accountability and transparency from members and CSOs alike, noting that accountability is not a one-way street with accountability required only of CSOs to members (lesson 11) (OECD, 2012, p. 43[7]). Relationships of accountability for results and for the ODA spent to achieve those results include CSO members, the beneficiaries and constituents of CSO programmes, and the publics in both member and partner countries. Transparency is needed in the processes and funding allocations of members and CSOs alike if CSOs are to avoid being seen as opaque or poorly managed.

Insights from the literature: Ongoing challenges and lessons

CSO accountability and perceptions of their accountability are critical to their effectiveness, whether as independent development actors or as implementers for members. Studies show there is disillusionment with CSOs due to actual and perceived accountability shortfalls. For example, the 2017 Edelman Trust Barometer found trust in NGOs dropped from the previous year (Edelman Holdings, 2017[78]).[29] There is a sense that CSOs are overly focused on the pursuit of funding opportunities and are losing touch with publics (Goldsmith, 2015[79]). These perceptions echo those reported in the 2011 Civil Society Index, which found CSOs were increasingly seen as lacking the legitimacy that derives from connection and solidarity with local partners and beneficiaries (CIVICUS, 2011[80]).

In the development co-operation domain, concern has grown over the tendency of CSOs to prioritise their relationship of upward accountability to their funders, which for a vast majority of CSOs are members.[30] Yet to build and maintain the public trust that is so critical to the legitimacy of individual CSOs and of the civil society sector, it is necessary to have effective CSOs that are invested in accountability at the partner country level where they work. This in turn can also strengthen the case against the type of regulatory restrictions by partner country governments that shrink the space for CSOs to operate.[31] In effect, CSO effectiveness, accountability and transparency can be seen as the "other side of the enabling environment coin" (Ceelen, Wood and Huesken, 2019, p. 13[39]).

Members' accountability focus tends to be directed towards home – to their institutions, wider governments and the public. Yet members cannot neglect accountability and transparency at partner country level. Paying attention to accountability and transparency at partner country level should begin with a solid understanding of the fact that how members support and engage with CSOs has the potential to negatively affect CSOs' accountability in partner countries. This study's discussion of members' financial support, administrative and results monitoring requirements, in particular, aims to help build this understanding.

CSOs' accountability needs strengthening in various ways. For example, the GPEDC 2019 progress report highlights the need for more and more inclusive co-ordination among CSOs, which not only helps to foster unity in the sector but can make interface with governments more effective while also reducing duplication (OECD/UNDP, 2019, pp. 67-68[30]). The use of participatory methods, empowerment-focused programming, constituency feedback and means such as human rights-based approaches can help to foster CSOs' accountability at partner country level (Ceelen, Wood and Huesken, 2019, pp. 26-34[39]). An important aspect of accountability in the current development landscape relates to prevention of sexual exploitation, abuse and harassment by CSO staff and volunteers. The 2019 DAC Recommendation on Ending Sexual Exploitation, Abuse, and Harassment in Development Co-operation and Humanitarian Assistance is a framework to support, guide and incentivise governments to take more robust action to prevent and respond to sexual exploitation, abuse and harassment, including in their capacity as donors (OECD DAC, 2019[81]). The Recommendation is intended to assist both members and implementing partners, including CSOs, to align their actions to prevent and respond to sexual exploitation, abuse and harassment. As the Recommendation is implemented and monitored, evidence and lessons will become available as to whether and how members' CSO partners are applying the Recommendation standards.[32]

Self-regulation is another important means for CSOs to address their accountability, individually and collectively. While it is the subject of considerable literature, there is limited member promotion. One resource for effective, self-managed CSO self-regulation is the Task Team's *2019 Guidance and Good Practice on CSO Development Effectiveness and Enabling Environment*, which includes tips on consultative design, monitoring for compliance and sanctioning of non-compliance (Ceelen, Wood and Huesken, 2019, p. 26[39]). Global-level initiatives promoting self-regulation include the Global Standard for CSO Accountability (Global Standard for CSO Accountability, n.d.[82]) and the Istanbul Principles for CSO Development Effectiveness (CSO Partnership for Development Effectiveness, 2018[83]). Literature that covers specific initiatives from which lessons can be drawn includes, among others, (Sidel, 2010[84]; Gugerty, 2010[85]; CSO Partnership for Development Effectiveness, 2016[86]) on various countries and (Prakash and Gugerty, 2010[87]) on various countries and sectors.

Members also need to demonstrate transparency at partner country level. The GPEDC 2019 progress report (OECD/UNDP, 2019[30]) shows there is considerable discrepancy between the perspectives of development partners, CSOs and governments on the extent to which development partners make information about their CSO support available to the public and to partner country governments. The perception is that information at the aggregate level of flows is made available more than details on partners, programmes and sectors, for example, with the majority of development partners not seen as making available information on their support for member country or international CSOs available (OECD/UNDP, 2019, pp. 136-137[30]).

These perspectives are echoed in a multi-member evaluation of support for civil society which concludes that detailed information about members' policies and support for CSOs tends to be neither available nor accessible at partner country level (Itad Ltd and COWI, 2012, p. 104[41]). While details on some funding flows should be treated with discretion to avoid placing CSO recipients that may be working on sensitive issues at risk in restrictive environments, greater transparency regarding flows would be beneficial. It could not only improve perceptions of member accountability and transparency at partner country level but might also lead to more positive perceptions of accountability of the CSOs that members support.

The International Aid Transparency Initiative (IATI) is sometimes touted as the solution to the transparency challenge. Although the number of CSOs reporting to IATI on the flows they receive from members is increasing, the dataset is currently not easily disaggregated to provide a picture of members' CSO flows, programmes and locations at partner country level (Ceelen, Wood and Huesken, 2019, p. 42[39]).[33]

In sum, implementation of accountability and transparency practices by CSOs and by members, especially focused at partner country level, is not simply the right thing to do but also an important strategy towards countering restrictions on CSOs. Lack of both accountability and of connection to partner country constituencies and publics leaves CSOs vulnerable. Members need to be more fully aware that they share some responsibility with CSOs for CSOs' accountability at partner country level and should ensure that the ways they support and engage with CSOs do no harm to CSOs' partner country-level accountability. Members would benefit from referring to the findings and action points of this study to self-assess whether their policies and practices of CSO support and engagement are as conducive as possible to reinforce CSOs' accountability at partner country level.

Moreover, members can support CSOs in numerous ways to strengthen their accountability, with emphasis on downward accountability at partner country level. These range from promoting CSO co-ordination and investing in CSO self-regulation to implementing standards of the DAC Recommendation on Ending Sexual Exploitation, Abuse, and Harassment in Development Co-operation and Humanitarian Assistance.

At the same time, transparency regarding members' country-specific flows for CSOs is a longstanding request of partner country stakeholders and particularly but not exclusively of partner country governments. However, such transparency is not sufficiently developed.

Chapter 2, building on this discussion of ongoing challenges in how members work with civil society, presents findings from the surveys of members and CSO networks conducted between November 2018 and March 2019.

References

Abrahamson, Z. et al. (2019), *Ensuring Civil Society is Heard: Principles and Practices to Improve Government Engagement with Civil Society*, Bond, London, https://www.bond.org.uk/sites/default/files/resource-documents/bond_ensuring_civil_societys_voice_is_heard-online_april_2019_update.pdf. [63]

Abuom, A. et al. (2012), *An Exploratory Study of the Wider Effects of Norwegian Civil Society Support to Countries in the South*, Norwegian Agency for Development Cooperation, Oslo, https://www.norad.no/globalassets/import-2162015-80434-am/www.norad.no-ny/filarkiv/vedlegg-til-publikasjoner/tracking-impact-an-exploratory-study-of-the-wider-effects-of-norwegian-civil-society-support-to-countries-in-the-south.pdf. [72]

ACT Alliance (2019), *Harmonization of Back Donor Requirements: Statement from European members of ACT Alliance*. [73]

Ariadne, International Human Rights Funders Group and European Foundation Centre (2015), *Challenging the Closing Space for Civil Society: A Practical Starting Point for Funders*, European Funders for Social Change and Human Rights (Ariadne), London, http://www.ariadne-network.eu/wp-content/uploads/2015/03/Ariadne_ClosingSpaceReport-Final-Version.pdf. [34]

Atia, M. and C. Herrold (2018), "Governing through patronage: The rise of NGOs and the fall of civil society in Palestine and Morocco", *Voluntas*, Vol. 29, http://dx.doi.org/10.1007/s11266-018-9953-6. [95]

Bisits Bullen, P. (2014), "Theory of change vs logical framework – What's the difference?", *Tools4dev - practical tools for international development blog*, http://www.tools4dev.org/resources/theory-of-change-vs-logical-framework-whats-the-difference-in-practice/ (accessed on 5 September 2019). [77]

Brusset, E. et al. (2017), *Evaluation: Programme-based Support through Finnish Civil Society Organizations II*, Ministry for Foreign Affairs of Finland, https://um.fi/documents/384998/385866/cso2_synthesis_report. [44]

Burger, R. and D. Seabe (2014), "NGO accountability in Africa", in Obadare, E. (ed.), *The Handbook of Civil Society in Africa*, Springer, London, https://link.springer.com/chapter/10.1007%2F978-1-4614-8262-8_6. [94]

Bushan, S. et al. (2018), "Putting the last first? Civil society's role in leaving no one behind", in *Development Co-operation Report 2018: Joining Forces to Leave No One Behind*, OECD Publishing, Paris, https://doi.org/10.1787/dcr-2018-en. [6]

Ceelen, A., J. Wood and S. Huesken (2019), *Guidance and Good Practice on CSO Development Effectiveness and Enabling Environment*, Task Team on CSO Development Effectiveness, The Hague, https://taskteamcso.com/wp-content/uploads/2019/04/TSKTM-01C-Guidance.pdf. [39]

CIVICUS (2015), *2015 State of Civil Society Report*, https://www.civicus.org/images/StateOfCivilSocietyFullReport2015.pdf. [42]

CIVICUS (2011), *Bridging the Gaps: Citizens, Organisations and Dissociation*, http://www.civicus.org/downloads/Bridging the Gaps - Citizens Organisations and Dissociation.pdf. [80]

Civil Society Summit (2019), *The Belgrade Call to Action*, http://aidwatchcanada.ca/wp-content/uploads/2019/04/Revised-April-Action-Agenda.pdf. [24]

Community of Democracies (2016), *Working Group on Enabling and Protecting Civil Society*, https://community-democracies.org/app/uploads/2016/10/09_28_2016_EPCS_One-Pager_FINAL.pdf. [32]

CONCORD (2017), *EU Delegations Report 2017: Towards a More Effective Partnership with CIvil Society*, https://concordeurope.org/wp-content/uploads/2017/03/CONCORD_EUDelegations_Report2017_EN.pdf. [70]

CONCORD Sweden (2018), *Make Space! Defending Civic Space and the Freedom of Association and Assembly*, https://concord.se/wp-content/uploads/2018/05/make-space-english-summary-2018-concord-sweden.pdf. [23]

CSO Partnership for Development Effectiveness (2018), *Istanbul Principles for CSO Development Effectiveness*, https://www.csopartnership.org/single-post/2018/02/15/Istanbul-Principles-for-CSO-Development-Effectiveness (accessed on 9 September 2019). [83]

CSO Partnership for Development Effectiveness (2016), *Istanbul Five Years After: Evidencing Civil Society Development Effectivness and Accountability*, http://edclibrary.csopartnership.org/bitstream/1/239/1/ISTANBUL-5.pdf. [86]

Department of Foreign Affairs and Trade of Australia (2015), *DFAT and NGOs: Effective Development Partners*, https://www.dfat.gov.au/sites/default/files/dfat-and-ngos-effective-development-partners.pdf. [18]

Department of Foreign Affairs and Trade of Australia and Coffey International Development (2015), *Evaluation of the Australian NGO Cooperation Program: Final Report*, https://dfat.gov.au/aid/how-we-measure-performance/ode/Documents/ode-evaluation-australian-ngo-cooperation-program-final-report.pdf. [17]

DFID (2016), *Civil Society Partnership Review*, United Kingdom Department for International Development (DFID), London, https://assets.publishing.service.gov.uk/government/uploads/system/uploads/attachment_data/file/565368/Civil-Society-Partnership-Review-3Nov2016.pdf. [48]

Ebrahim, A. (2003), "Accountability in practice: Mechanisms for NGOs", *World Development*, Vol. 31/5, pp. 813-829, https://doi.org/10.1016/S0305-750X(03)00014-7. [96]

Edelman Holdings (2017), *2017 Edelman Trust Barometer: Executive Summary*, https://www.scribd.com/document/336621519/2017-Edelman-Trust-Barometer-Executive-Summary. [78]

Edwards, M. (2011), "Introduction: Civil society and the geometry of human relations", in Edwards, M. (ed.), *The Oxford Handbook of Civil Society*, Oxford University Press, New York, NY. [8]

Edwards, M. (2009), *Civil Society - Second Edition*, Polity Press, Cambridge, UK. [10]

Franklin, J. (2017), "Editorial", *The Foundation Review*, Vol. 9/3, pp. 2-5, https://scholarworks.gvsu.edu/cgi/viewcontent.cgi?article=1382&context=tfr. [91]

Garcia, C. (2016), *PFD Review 2016: Executive Summary*, European Commission, Brussels, https://europa.eu/capacity4dev/policy-forum-development/document/pfd-review-2016-executive-summary-en. [65]

Global Standard for CSO Accountability (n.d.), *Guidance Material (web page)*, http://www.csostandard.org/guidance-material/ (accessed on 9 September 2019). [82]

Goldsmith, B. (2015), "Why is trust in NGOs falling?", *World Economic Forum - Agenda: Infrastructure blog*, https://www.weforum.org/agenda/2015/01/why-is-trust-in-ngos-falling/. [79]

GPEDC (2018), *2018 Monitoring Guide for National Co-ordinators from Participating Governments*, Global Partnership for Effective Development Co-operation (GPEDC), Paris, http://effectivecooperation.org/pdf/2018_Monitoring_Guide_National_Coordinator.pdf. [93]

GPEDC (2018), *Indicator 2 Questionnaire - Characteristics of Practice*, Global Partnership for Effective Development Co-operation (GPEDC), Paris, https://www.dropbox.com/s/g5bvf6whstwl7md/Indicator%202%20Characteristics%20of%20practice%20CLEAN.pdf.   [14]

GPEDC (2016), *Nairobi Outcome Document*, Global Partnership for Effective Development Co-operation (GPEDC), Paris, http://effectivecooperation.org/wp-content/uploads/2016/12/OutcomeDocumentEnglish.pdf.   [27]

Gugerty, M. (2010), "The emergence of nonprofit self-regulation in Africa", *Nonprofit and Voluntary Sector Quarterly*, Vol. 39/6, pp. 1087-1112, http://dx.doi.org/10.1177/0899764010372972.   [85]

Haynes, R., V. Ireland and J. Duke (2019), *Funding Civil Society Organisations & Networks: Promising Approaches to Financing Development in the 21st Century*, Forus, Paris, http://forus-international.org/en/resources/71.   [43]

Hogg, A. and R. Hodess (2018), *The Business Case for Protecting Civic Rights*, The B Team, New York, https://bteam.org/assets/reports/The-Business-Case-for-Protecting-Civic-Rights.pdf.   [35]

Howell, J. and J. Hall (2012), *Working Beyond Government: Evaluation of AusAID's Engagement with Civil Society in Developing Countries*, Australian Agency for International Development, Canberra, http://www.oecd.org/derec/49905692.pdf.   [50]

Hulme, D. and M. Edwards (1997), "NGOs, states and donors: An overview", in Hulme, D. and M. Edwards (eds.), *NGOs, states and donors: Too close for comfort?*, Palgrave Macmillan, U.K, https://www.palgrave.com/gp/book/9781137355140.   [4]

Inter-Agency Standing Committee (2020), *Harmonize and simplify reporting requirements (web page)*, United Nations Office for the Coordination of Humanitarian Affairs, New York/Geneva, https://interagencystandingcommittee.org/harmonize-and-simplify-reporting-requirements.   [69]

Inter-Agency Standing Committee (2020), *More support and funding tools for local and national responders (web page)*, United Nations Office for the Coordination of Humanitarian Affairs, New York/Geneva, https://interagencystandingcommittee.org/more-support-and-funding-tools-for-local-and-national-responders.   [51]

International Center for Not-for-Profit Law (2018), *Effective Donor Responses to the Challenge of Closing Civic Space*, https://www.hrfn.org/wp-content/uploads/2018/06/Effective-donor-responses-FINAL-1-May-2018.pdf.   [25]

INTRAC (2014), *Study on Support to Civil Society through Multi-Donor Funds*, https://www.intrac.org/wpcms/wp-content/uploads/2016/09/Study_on_Support_to_Civil_Society_through_Multi-Donor_Funds.pdf.   [59]

INTRAC (2013), "Support to civil society: Emerging evaluation lessons", *Evaluation Insights*, No. 8, OECD Publishing, Paris, http://www.oecd.org/dac/evaluation/Evaluation%20Insight%20Civil%20Society%20FINAL%20for%20print%20and%20WEB%2020131004.pdf.   [58]

INTRAC and Ministry of Foreign Affairs of Denmark (2014), *Multi-Donor Funds in Support of Civil Society: A Guidance Note for Danish Missions*, https://amg.um.dk/policies-and-strategies/policy-for-support-to-danish-civil-society/guidance-note/. [61]

IOD PARC (2017), *Independent Evaluation of SDC Partnerships with Swiss NGOs*, Swiss Agency for Development Cooperation, Bern, https://www.newsd.admin.ch/newsd/NSBExterneStudien/834/attachment/de/3524.pdf. [20]

Itad Ltd and COWI (2012), *Support to Civil Society Engagement in Policy Dialogue: Synthesis Report*, Ministry of Foreign Affairs of Denmark, https://itad.com/wp-content/uploads/2013/02/evaluation_synthesis_report.pdf. [41]

Karlstedt, C. et al. (2015), *Effectiveness of Core Funding to CSOs in the Field of Human Rights and International Humanitarian Law in Occupied Palestine*, Swedish International Development Cooperation Agency (Sida), Stockholm, https://www.sida.se/contentassets/45bc6fdacc9b464bae3b89cd041c4cbe/15934.pdf. [49]

Kohler-Koch, B. and C. Quittkat (2009), "What is civil society and who represents civil society in the EU?-Results of an online survey among civil society experts", *Policy and Society*, Vol. 28/1, pp. 11-22, http://dx.doi.org/10.1016/j.polsoc.2009.02.002. [9]

Ljungman, C. and A. Nilsson (2018), *Icelandic CSO Evaluation: Synthesis Report*, Government of Iceland, Reykjavík, https://www.stjornarradid.is/lisalib/getfile.aspx?itemid=c94f173e-e2a3-11e8-942d-005056bc530c. [55]

McGillivray, M. et al. (2018), *Evaluation of MFAT's Partnerships Fund*, New Zealand Ministry of Foreign Affairs and Trade, Wellington, https://www.mfat.govt.nz/assets/Aid-Prog-docs/Evaluations/2018/MFAT-Partnerships-Fund-Evaluation-Report-March-2018.pdf. [71]

Ministry for Foreign Affairs of Finland (2015), *Results Based Management (RBM) in Finland's Development Cooperation: Concepts and Guiding Principles*. [76]

Molenaers, N., J. Faust and S. Dellepiane (2015), "Political conditionality and foreign aid", *World Development*, Vol. 75, pp. 2-12, https://doi.org/10.1016/j.worlddev.2015.04.001. [22]

National Audit Office (2006), *Department for International Development: Working with Non-Governmental and Other Civil Society Organisations to Promote Development*, https://www.nao.org.uk/wp-content/uploads/2006/07/05061311.pdf. [46]

Nilsson, A. et al. (2013), *Review of Civil Society Support Modalities at Sida HQ and Swedish Embassies: Final Report*, Swedish International Development Cooperation Agency (Sida), Stockholm, https://www.sida.se/contentassets/a3dc882f93664d85bcde92d336f1a749/review-of-civil-society-support-modalities-at-sida-hq-and-swedish-embassies---final-report_3475.pdf. [40]

OECD (2020), *Creditor Reporting System (database)*, https://stats.oecd.org/Index.aspx?DataSetCode=crs1. [2]

OECD (2020), "Digital transformation and the futures of civic space to 2030", *Foresight Policy Papers*, OECD Publishing, Paris. [36]

OECD (2019), *Aid for Civil Society Organisations*, OECD, Paris, https://www.oecd.org/dac/financing-sustainable-development/development-finance-topics/Aid-for-CSOs-2019.pdf. [97]

OECD (2019), *Peer Review Synthesis Note: Civil Society (unpublished)*, OECD Publishing, Paris. [16]

OECD (2018), *Development Co-operation Report 2018: Joining Forces to Leave No One Behind*, OECD Publishing, Paris, https://dx.doi.org/10.1787/dcr-2018-en. [92]

OECD (2017), *Recommendation of the Council on Open Government*, OECD Publishing, Paris, https://www.oecd.org/gov/Recommendation-Open-Government-Approved-Council-141217.pdf. [62]

OECD (2014), *Engaging with the Public: 12 Lessons from DAC Peer Reviews and the Network of DAC Development Communicators*, OECD Publishing, Paris, https://www.oecd.org/dac/peer-reviews/12%20Lessons%20Engaging%20with%20the%20public.pdf. [90]

OECD (2012), *Partnering with Civil Society: 12 Lessons from DAC Peer Reviews*, OECD Development Co-operation Peer Reviews, OECD Publishing, Paris, https://dx.doi.org/10.1787/9789264200173-en. [7]

OECD (2011), *Busan Partnership for Effective Development Co-operation*, OECD Publishing, Paris, https://www.oecd.org/development/effectiveness/busanpartnership.htm. [3]

OECD (2011), *How DAC Members Work with Civil Society Organisations: An Overview*, OECD Publishing, Paris, http://www.oecd.org/dac/peer-reviews/Final_How_DAC_members_work_with_CSOs_ENGLISH.pdf. [88]

OECD (2010), *Civil Society and Aid Effectiveness: Findings, Recommendations and Good Practice*, Better Aid, OECD Publishing, Paris, https://dx.doi.org/10.1787/9789264056435-en. [5]

OECD DAC (2019), *DAC Peer Review Reference Guide, 2019-20*, OECD Publishing, Paris, https://www.oecd.org/dac/peer-reviews/DAC-peer-review-reference-guide.pdf. [15]

OECD DAC (2019), "DAC Recommendation on Ending Sexual Exploitation, Abuse, and Harassment in Development Co-operation and Humanitarian Assistance: Key Pillars of Prevention and Response", No. OECD/LEGAL/5020, OECD Publishing, Paris, https://legalinstruments.oecd.org/en/instruments/OECD-LEGAL-5020. [81]

OECD DAC (2019), "DAC Recommendation on the Humanitarian-Development-Peace Nexus", OECD Publishing, Paris, https://legalinstruments.oecd.org/en/instruments/OECD-LEGAL-5019. [31]

OECD DAC (2019), *Ensuring Effective and Quality Support for the Multlateral System*, OECD Publishing, Paris. [38]

OECD DAC (2018), "Converged statistical reporting directives for the Creditor Reporting System (CRS) and the annual DAC Questionnaire", No. DCD/DAC/STAT(2018)9/FINAL, OECD Publishing, Paris, https://one.oecd.org/document/DCD/DAC/STAT(2018)9/FINAL/en/pdf. [13]

OECD DAC (2018), "Framework for dialogue between the DAC and civil society organisations", No. DCD/DAC(2018)28/FINAL, OECD Publishing, Paris, http://www.oecd.org/officialdocuments/publicdisplaydocumentpdf/?cote=DCD/DAC(2018)28/FINAL&docLanguage=En. [66]

OECD/European Union (2017), *Boosting Social Enterprise Development: Good Practice Compendium*, OECD Publishing, Paris, https://doi.org/10.1787/9789264268500-en. [12]

OECD/UNDP (2019), *Making Development Co-operation More Effective: 2019 Progress Report*, OECD Publishing, Paris, https://doi.org/10.1787/26f2638f-en. [30]

OECD/UNDP (2016), *Making Development Co-operation More Effective: 2016 Progress Report*, OECD Publishing, Paris, https://doi.org/10.1787/9789264266261-en. [53]

Open Government Partnership (2019), *Open Government Partnership Global Report: Executive Summary*, https://www.opengovpartnership.org/wp-content/uploads/2019/05/Global-Report_Executive-Summary_EN.pdf. [33]

Prakash, A. and M. Gugerty (2010), "Trust but verify? Voluntary regulation programs in the nonprofit sector", *Regulation & Governance*, Vol. 4/1, pp. 22-47, http://dx.doi.org/10.1111/j.1748-5991.2009.01067.x. [87]

Salamon, L. (2010), "Putting the civil society sector on the economic map of the world", *Annals of Public and Cooperative Economics*, Vol. 81/2, pp. 167-210, http://dx.doi.org/10.1111/j.1467-8292.2010.00409.x. [1]

Sida (2019), *Guiding Principles for Sida's Engagement with and Support to Civil Society*, Swedish International Development Cooperation Agency (Sida), Stockholm, https://www.sida.se/contentassets/86933109610e48929d76764121b63fc6/10202931_guiding_principle_2019_no_examples_web.pdf. [37]

Sidel, M. (2010), "The promise and limits of collective action for nonprofit self-regulation: Evidence from Asia", *Nonprofit and Voluntary Sector Quarterly*, Vol. 39/6, pp. 1039-1056, http://dx.doi.org/10.1177/0899764010371514. [84]

Smith, S. (2010), "Hybridization and nonprofit organizations: The governance challenge", *Policy and Society*, Vol. 29/3, pp. 219-229, https://doi.org/10.1016/j.polsoc.2010.06.003. [11]

Sogge, D. (2019), "Is civic space really shrinking, and if so who's to blame?", https://www.opendemocracy.net/en/transformation/is-civic-space-really-shrinking-and-if-so-whos-to-blame/ (accessed on 24 September 2019). [57]

Stage, O. et al. (2016), *Evaluation: Programme-based Support through Finnish Civil Society Organizations*, Ministry for Foreign Affairs of Finland, https://um.fi/documents/384998/385866/cso1_evaluation_synthesis_report/f096acb8-d351-1722-5e31-6f656e7b04a5?t=1528280881371. [64]

Staniforth, S. (2009), *Providing Core Funding to Non-Profits: A Review of the Research Landscape and the Pilot Stewardship Works! Initiative*, Stewardship Centre of BC, Campbell River, British Columbia, http://www.stewardshipcentrebc.ca/PDF_docs/SW/Stewardship_Works_Report_on_Core_Funding_2009_SCBC.pdf. [47]

Suarez, D. and M. Gugerty (2016), "Funding civil society? Bilateral government support for development NGOs", *Voluntas*, Vol. 27/6, pp. 2617-2649, https://doi.org/10.1007/s11266-016-9706-3. [52]

Swiss Agency for Development and Cooperation (2019), *SDC Guidance for Engagement with Swiss NGOs*, https://www.eda.admin.ch/dam/deza/en/documents/publikationen/Diverses/richtlinien-zusammenarbeit-schweizer-NGO_EN.pdf. [19]

Task Team on CSO Development Effectiveness and Enabling Environment (2014), *Review of Evidence: Progress on Civil Society-related Commitments of the Busan High Level Forum*, https://taskteamcso.com/wp-content/uploads/2019/04/Task-Team-Review-of-Evidence.pdf. [74]

Tjønneland, E. et al. (2018), *From Donors to Partners? Evaluation of Norwegian Support to Strengthen Civil Society in Developing Countries through Norwegian Civil Society Organisations*, Norwegian Agency for Development Cooperation, Oslo, https://norad.no/globalassets/filer-2017/evaluering/1.18-from-donor-to-partners/1.18-from-donors-to-partners_main-report.pdf. [54]

UN (2018), *Guidelines for States on the Effective Implementation of the Right to Participate in Public Affairs*, Office of the United Nations High Commissioner for Human Rights, New York, https://www.ohchr.org/Documents/Issues/PublicAffairs/GuidelinesRightParticipatePublicAffairs_web.pdf. [67]

UN (2017), "Report of the Special Rapporteur on the rights to freedom of peaceful assembly and of association", No. A/HRC/35/28, United Nations General Assembly, New York, http://freeassembly.net/wp-content/uploads/2017/05/A.HRC_.35.28.English.pdf. [26]

Vähämäki, J. and C. Verger (2019), "Learning from results-based management evaluations and reviews", *OECD Development Co-operation Working Papers*, No. 53, OECD Publishing, Paris, https://doi.org/10.1787/3fda0081-en. [75]

Van Rooy, A. (2004), *The Global Legitimacy Game: Civil Society, Globalization and Protest*, Palgrave MacMillan, New York, NY. [28]

Wayne-Nixon, L. et al. (2019), *Effective Multi-Stakeholder Engagement to Realize the 2030 Agenda*, British Columbia Council for International Cooperation/Canadian Council for International Co-operation, Vancouver/Ottawa, https://ccic.ca/wp-content/uploads/2019/04/Effective_Engagement_International.pdf. [68]

Wood, J. (2019), *State and Self-regulation of Civil Society Organizations in Context: A Case Study of Kenya (unpublished doctoral dissertation)*, Carleton University, Ottawa, Canada, http://dx.doi.org/doi:10.22215/etd/2019-m17011. [21]

Wood, J. (2016), "Unintended consequences: DAC governments and shrinking civil society space in Kenya", *Development in Practice*, Vol. 26/5, pp. 532-543, http://dx.doi.org/10.1080/09614524.2016.1188882. [89]

Wood, J. and K. Fällman (2019), "Enabling civil society: Select survey findings", *OECD Development Co-operation Working Papers*, No. 57, OECD Publishing, Paris, https://dx.doi.org/10.1787/54903a6a-en. [60]

Wood, J. and K. Fällman (2013), "Official donors' engagement with civil society: Key issues in 2012", in *State of Civil Society 2013: Creating an Enabling Environment - The Synthesis Report*, CIVICUS, Johannesburg, https://reliefweb.int/sites/reliefweb.int/files/resources/2013StateofCivilSocietyReport_full.pdf. [45]

World Movement for Democracy Secretariat and International Center for Not-for-Profit Law (2012), *Defending Civil Society - Second Edition*, https://www.icnl.org/post/report/defending-civil-society-report-second-edition. [29]

Youngs, R. (2015), *Rethinking Civil Society and Support for Democracy*, Expert Group for Aid Studies, Stockholm, https://eba.se/wp-content/uploads/2015/04/Rapport-2015-01-med-framsida_f%C3%B6r_web.pdf. [56]

Notes

[1] These calculations are based on 2017 constant prices.

[2] The OECD figure on private contributions from CSOs is considered to under-represent the total amount of such contributions, as the figures are reported not from CSOs themselves but from DAC members. See (OECD, 2011, p. 10[88]) at http://www.oecd.org/dac/peer-reviews/Final_How_DAC_members_work_with_CSOs_ENGLISH.pdf.

[3] These commitments are reflected in the GPEDC monitoring framework Indicator 2: CSOs operate within an environment that maximises their engagement in and contribution to development. See (GPEDC, 2018[93]) at http://effectivecooperation.org/pdf/2018_Monitoring_Guide_National_Coordinator.pdf.

[4] 1Part IAnnex A presents additional information on sources and methods used for this study.

[5] The civil society sector is referred to variously as the non-profit sector, the voluntary sector, the third sector, or the non-governmental organisation or NGO sector.

[6] For additional discussion on informality and fluidity, see Youngs (2015[56]) at https://eba.se/wp-content/uploads/2015/04/Rapport-2015-01-med-framsida_f%C3%B6r_web.pdf. See also Smith (2010[11]) on "hybridization" at https://doi.org/10.1016/j.polsoc.2010.06.003.

[7] See, for example, Franklin (2017[91]) for a summary discussion of the rise of community foundations and philanthropy that mobilise human and financial capital towards improving lives and livelihoods, at https://scholarworks.gvsu.edu/cgi/viewcontent.cgi?article=1382&context=tfr.

[8] See, for example, the OECD (2019[97]) report regarding aid for CSOs at https://www.oecd.org/dac/financing-sustainable-development/development-finance-topics/Aid-for-CSOs-2019.pdf. Also see the OECD (2018[92]) *Development Co-operation Report* at https://dx.doi.org/10.1787/dcr-2018-en.

[9] The surveys conducted for this study and the study itself use the term "partner country" to denote a country receiving official development assistance. The term "developing country" is occasionally used in this document when a source uses that term. For example, DAC reporting directives refer to developing country-based NGOs.

[10] Partner country-based CSOs can also play this intermediary, donor-type role, although this role is typical for member country-based and international CSOs.

[11] On the issue of civic space and technology, see the OECD (2020[36]) Foresight Policy Paper, "Digital transformation and the futures of civic space to 2030".

[12] It is widely recognised that not all of civil society or all CSOs hold and/or operate by what might be considered positive social values. See, for instance, OECD (2010, p. 26[5]) at https://dx.doi.org/10.1787/9789264056435-en; Edwards (2009, pp. 53-54[10]); and paragraph 3 in Sogge (2019[57]) at https://www.opendemocracy.net/en/transformation/is-civic-space-really-shrinking-and-if-so-whos-to-blame/. However, this is often forgotten in the discussion on civil society and CSOs in development co-operation. Legitimacy claims cannot be based on normative values alone.

[13] Note that GPEDC monitoring assesses progress of what it refers to as development partners, which include not only DAC members but also multilateral development banks, UN agencies and other development co-operation providers.

[14] The OECD (2014, p. 39[90]) publication, *Engaging with the Public: 12 Lessons from DAC Peer Reviews and the Network of DAC Development Communicators*, encourages members to leverage partnerships to convey development messages, pointing to CSOs as important strategic partners in this task. See https://www.oecd.org/dac/peer-reviews/12%20Lessons%20Engaging%20with%20the%20public.pdf.

[15] Monitoring of the DAC Recommendation on the Humanitarian-Development-Peace Nexus will primarily be undertaken through the existing DAC peer review mechanism and supplemented by case studies and the sharing of good practice through the DAC's subsidiary body, the International Network on Conflict and Fragility (OECD DAC, 2019, p. 11[31]).

[16] This perspective is largely shared by partner country governments, though development partners' inputs paint a different picture of much greater availability of funding that is either core support or is co-defined between CSOs and development partners. See Part II, page 134, of the GPEDC *2019 Progress Report* at https://doi.org/10.1787/26f2638f-en.

[17] This evaluation was initiated by the International Donor Group on Civil Society and was commissioned by three of the group's members: Danida, the Austrian Development Agency and Sida.

[18] This issue is common to core support for institutions other than CSOs. Members have raised similar concerns about core support to multilateral institutions, for instance reporting that with less ability to be directive in their funding for multilaterals, they are less able to measure results achieved. See (OECD DAC, 2019, p. 6[31]) at https://legalinstruments.oecd.org/public/doc/643/643.en.pdf.

[19] Calls for proposals are rarely used to administer core support *to* CSOs.

[20] Launched in 2016, the Grand Bargain is an agreement among the largest funders and humanitarian aid organisations to improve the efficiency and effectiveness of humanitarian action.

[21] The *Progress Report* is based on submissions from partner country-level actors (e.g. governments, CSOs, members and other official donors including multilateral agencies). Its findings therefore do not reflect what members might be doing to engage CSOs in dialogue in member countries.

[22] The European Union's dialogue to develop civil society roadmaps, discussed in Chapter 3, is an example of dialogue co-ordination.

[23] Abrahamson et al. (2019[63]) cite the United Kingdom government's preoccupation with Brexit as an additional, significant impediment to DFID-CSO dialogue. See https://www.bond.org.uk/sites/default/files/resource-documents/bond_ensuring_civil_societys_voice_is_heard-online_april_2019_update.pdf.

[24] Note that the research for the working paper drew not only on member evaluations and reviews but also those of multilateral agencies. See (Vähämäki and Verger, 2019[75]) at http://www.oecd.org/dac/results-development/docs/Results-Workshop-Learning-from-RBM-evaluations-FINAL.pdf.

[25] For information on the Thinking and Working Politically Community of Practice, see https://twpcommunity.org. A discussion of the Global Learning for Adaptive Management and Doing Development Differently initiatives is available at https://www.odi.org/projects/2918-global-learning-adaptive-management-initiative-glam.

[26] The Oxfam From Poverty to Power blog is at https://oxfamblogs.org/fp2p/. See also a report on Christian Aid's experience with adaptive management at https://www.odi.org/sites/odi.org.uk/files/resource-documents/12387.pdf.

[27] See https://scholarworks.gvsu.edu/tfr/.

[28] The M&E Universe webpage is at https://embed.kumu.io/4130478e59248ce0f8871377a7fb7c4e#me-universe.

[29] Though NGOs remained the most trusted institution, their trust ranking was virtually the same as that of business and higher than media and government.

[30] See, among others, (Ebrahim, 2003[96]) at https://doi.org/10.1016/S0305-750X(03)00014-7; (Burger and Seabe, 2014[94]) at https://link.springer.com/chapter/10.1007%2F978-1-4614-8262-8_6; and (Atia and Herrold, 2018[95]) at https://doi.org/10.1007/s11266-018-9953-6.

[31] Issues related to how members' policies and practices affect partner country governments' attitude towards and treatment of CSOs, beyond a discussion of how members support CSOs, are beyond the remit of this study. These issues include the changing geopolitical landscape, and thus the degree of members' policy influence, and increasingly competing priorities such as investment and trade relative to human rights and democratisation. See, for example, (Wood, 2016[89]) at https://doi.org/10.1080/09614524.2016.1188882 and (Wood, 2019[21]) at https://doi.org/10.22215/etd/2019-m17011.

[32] An Action Plan for such monitoring is under development by the OECD Development Co-operation Directorate's Gender Equality and Women's Empowerment Team in its work with the DAC Network on Gender Equality (GenderNet). Monitoring will be done with a multi-stakeholder group, the DAC Reference Group on Preventing Sexual Exploitation, Abuse and Harassment. The Action Plan on Monitoring and Learning to Support Implementation of the DAC Recommendation on Ending Sexual Exploitation, Abuse, and Harassment in Development Co-operation and Humanitarian Assistance includes a menu of monitoring and learning areas. Among these are peer learning workshops on key pillars, voluntary reviews, a toolkit for reform, regular surveys of member progress, and the existing DAC peer review mechanism. More in-depth and frequent monitoring and review were agreed upon within the first five years following adoption of the Recommendation. The Recommendation is available at https://legalinstruments.oecd.org/en/instruments/OECD-LEGAL-5020.

[33] According to the IATI dashboard, as of September 2019, more than 670 NGOs were reporting to IATI, approximately 100 more than were reporting in October 2018. See the IATI dashboard Summary Statistics at http://publishingstats.iatistandard.org/summary_stats.html#h_narrative.

2 Working with civil society: Findings from surveys and consultations

This chapter presents a comprehensive picture of how members and civil society organisations (CSOs) work together. It draws on responses of members and CSOs to two separate surveys conducted over 2018 and 2019; members' policy documents that are relevant to their work with civil society; and feedback from online and in-person consultations with both members and CSOs. This analysis of how members work with civil society suggests there is room for improvement and a need for guidance to better equip members to enable civil society and CSOs to maximise their contributions to development.

2.1. How members define CSOs and civil society

Key findings

There is considerable commonality across members' definitions of a civil society organisation (CSO). There are also differences, especially in the degree to which the diversity of civil society actors is reflected in definitions. Civil society is rarely defined.

The survey of members asked *how does your institution define CSOs and civil society?*[1] Members provided quite varied responses.[2] Two members (Australia, Canada) cite the definition in the OECD (2010[1]) report, *Civil Society and Aid Effectiveness: Findings, Recommendations and Good Practice*. This definition is also used in the OECD (2011, p. 10[2]) report, *How DAC Members Work with Civil Society Organisations: An Overview*. The Swiss Agency for Development and Cooperation (SDC) refers to the DAC definition in the OECD (2018, p. 2[3]) report, *Aid for Civil Society Organisations*, and also in DAC reporting directives. The United States Agency for International Development (USAID) does not have a corporate definition of civil society but cites the definition of a CSO developed by Johns Hopkins University as an organisation that is separate from government, non-profit distributing, self-governing, formal or informal and in which participation is voluntary. Some recurring themes in members' definitions that reflect the Johns Hopkins University definition are that CSOs are distinct from the state and the private sector and that they are non-profit organisations. A few members (Canada, Germany, Iceland, Ireland), specifically state that voluntarism is a distinguishing feature of CSOs. For other members, voluntarism is implicit in the concept of CSOs as a coming together of people (or citizens) on a voluntary basis in the pursuit of shared objectives, interests or ideals.

The CSO definitions of Belgium, Italy and Spain are enshrined in their laws on development co-operation. Italian Law 125/2014 (Italian Agency for Development Cooperation, 2014[4]) sets out six categories of CSOs that are considered part of the Italian development co-operation system, inclusive of a category dedicated to a category of Italian CSOs awarded advisor status at the United Nations (UN) Economic and Social Council in the previous four years. Spanish Law 23/1998 stipulates that in order to receive official aid funds, CSOs must be registered under the Registry of Non-Governmental Organizations of Development (Government of Spain, 2014[5]). A non-governmental development organisation (NGDO) is further defined as an organisation that includes, as one of its purposes, promotion of the principles and objectives of international co-operation as stipulated in Law 23/1998. Article 2 of the Belgian Law on Development Co-operation defines a CSO as a "non-state and non-profit entity in which people organize themselves to pursue common goals or ideals" (Government of Belgium, 2013[6]).[3] CSOs applying for funding from some of Belgium's support mechanisms must demonstrate that they meet the CSO definition in the Law on Development Co-operation as well as criteria in the Royal Decree of 11 September 2016 on non-governmental co-operation (Government of Belgium, 2016[7]).

As discussed in Section 1.2, many types of organisations are considered to be CSOs, and this is reflected in members' definitions of CSOs and how they refer to them in policy documents. Examples of CSO types are at times specific to the individuals, communities or causes represented. These include diaspora or migrant organisations (Belgium); gender and lesbian, gay, bisexual and transgender organisations (European Commission (EC)); and NGDOs (Belgium and Portugal). Some organisations fall in a grey area, considered CSOs by some members but not so by others. Research and academic institutions, for example, are a separate organisational category for some members including Belgium and the French Development Agency (AFD). Occasionally, a member's CSO definition includes non-formal associations of civil society (EC, Czech Republic, USAID). Members' CSO definitions also commonly refer to the activity arenas – e.g. cultural, environmental, social and economic, civic and political – engaged in by the CSO. Two members (EC, Spain) specify the non-partisan nature of CSOs and their activities.

A distinction between civil society and CSOs is not always made in members' policies or survey responses. For many, civil society seems to be understood as the collection of CSOs. For others, civil society is seen as a broader sphere of human activity (Finland); of initiatives and social movements (Germany, Canada, Ireland); and of the individuals engaging in this sphere such as volunteers, artists or journalists (Czech Republic).

In sum, the way members define and refer to CSOs has much in common with the OECD and DAC definitions of CSOs and non-governmental organisations (NGOs) as non-profit, non-state entities in which people organise to pursue common interests (Section 1.2). However, there are also considerable differences. These differences may lead to confusion across members. The differences also suggest that some members are more inclusive in the range of civil society actors that they support and engage with. The broader concept of civil society is rarely defined.

2.2. Member CSO and/or civil society policies

Key findings

- There is considerable variation in the types of document that members consider to be a policy for working with CSOs and/or civil society, and these include legislation, policies, strategies, guidelines, principles and action plans.
- Most members (22 respondents) have some form of policy covering CSOs and/or civil society and for 16 of these, their policy is specific to either CSOs and/or civil society.
- Three members indicate they are developing policies and four indicate they do not have a policy.
- Policies are being developed in consultation with CSOs, and some members involve CSOs in policy monitoring.
- Integration of civil society-related issues across other policies, inclusive of but even beyond development and foreign policy, is insufficiently addressed by members.

According to survey responses, the majority of members (22, 76%) have in place some form of *policy/strategy for working with CSOs and/or civil society*.[4,5,6,7] The type of document that members consider to be a policy for working with CSOs and/or civil society varies. Some have CSO and/or civil society-specific policies in the form of legislation (e.g. Portugal's NGDO Charter), multi-year or annual plans (e.g. Poland), policies (e.g. Canada), strategies (e.g. Germany), principles (e.g. Swedish International Development Cooperation Agency (Sida)), or guidelines (e.g. Finland).

Of the 22 members that indicated they have a policy, 22 (73%) refer to a document specific to CSOs and/or civil society in development. For instance, the Netherlands' 2014 CSO policy, *Dialogue and Dissent*, is not only CSO-specific but is exclusive to partnerships with CSOs in a lobbying and advocacy role (Government of the Netherlands, 2014[8]). The policies referred to by 6 of these 22 members are broader development policies that also address CSOs and/or civil society.

Three members indicate they are developing policies. Irish Aid, for example, is updating its 2008 policy, with completion anticipated in 2019. The Spanish Agency for International Development Cooperation (AECID) 2018-21 master plan for development co-operation commits to elaborating a strategy for collaboration with CSOs (Government of Spain, 2018[9]). In the case of Belgium, the Royal Decree of 11 September 2016 addresses the practical and political implementation of Belgium's support for CSOs in development co-operation and, combined with a theory of change for this support under finalisation, will make up Belgium's CSO policy (Government of Belgium, 2016[7]).

Another four members indicate that they do not have a CSO and/or civil society policy. Of these, New Zealand is revisiting its approach to CSOs following a 2018 evaluation, while Hungary does not indicate that a policy is planned for. The Norwegian Agency for Development Cooperation (Norad) (2018[10]) published "guiding principles" for its support for civil society. But because Norad does not have the authority to make policy per se, Norway considers it does not have a specific CSO and/or civil society policy. However, partnership with civil society is covered in overall development policies including the central white paper of 2017, *Common Responsibility for Common Future: The Sustainable Development Goals and Norway's Development Policy* (Norwegian Ministry of Foreign Affairs, 2017[11]). Similarly, USAID indicates that it does not have a CSO and/or civil society-specific policy. However, the importance of civil society and CSOs is recognised in various sector-specific policies as well as in broad government policies that guide USAID's programming. Box 2.1 presents a summary of member responses.

Box 2.1. Members with CSO or civil society policies

Findings from member responses to the survey include the following:

- 22 members indicate they have some form of CSO and/or civil society policy
- of the 22 members indicating they have some form of CSO and/or civil society policy, 16 of the policies are CSO and/or civil society-specific
- 3 members indicate they are developing policies
- 4 members indicate they do not have a policy.

Note: Findings are drawn from member policies provided in response to the How DAC Members Work with Civil Society survey of members, conducted between November 2018 and March 2019.

Some members that do not have a CSO and/or civil society-specific policy say in their survey responses that they have a policy. These members consider the coverage of CSOs and civil society in broader legislative or policy documents or in sector-specific policies as providing adequate coverage to constitute a CSO policy. Thus, based on their survey responses, these members are included among the 22 having a CSO or civil society policy. They tend to be newer members and/or those with smaller official development assistance (ODA) budgets than longer-standing members. Poland, for example, refers to its CSO policy as being covered within the *Multiannual Development Cooperation Programme 2016-2020* (Ministry of Foreign Affairs of Poland, 2015[12]) and associated annual plans. For Luxembourg, coverage of CSOs in its 1996 Law on Development Cooperation, together with amendments to the law in 2012 and 2017 addressing CSO partnerships, constitute its CSO policy (Government of the Grandy Duchy of Luxembourg, 1996[13]; Government of the Grand Duchy of Luxembourg, 2012[14]; Government of the Grand Duchy of Luxembourg, 2017[15]). This is further supported by CSO coverage in its 2018 development co-operation strategy, *The Road to 2030* (Government of the Grand Duchy of Luxembourg, 2018[16]).

Having a CSO-specific policy does not preclude coverage of CSOs and/or civil society in wider development co-operation or in sector-specific policies (or legislation) as well. The EC communication, *The Roots of Democracy and Sustainable Development: Europe's Engagement with Civil Society in External Relations* (European Commission, 2012[17]), is complemented by the 2017 *New European Consensus on Development* (European Commission, 2017[18]). The Czech Republic considers all or parts of several official documents as constituting its CSO policy: its annual Resolution on Main Areas of State Subsidy Policy Towards Non-governmental Non-profit Organisations (which covers all NGOs supported by the Czech government, not solely those involved in development co-operation) and reference to these actors in its 2018-30 *International Development Cooperation Strategy*, the *Human Rights and Transition Policy*

Strategy and the annual *Humanitarian Assistance Strategy* (Ministry of Foreign Affairs of the Czech Republic, 2017[19]; Ministry of Foreign Affairs of the Czech Republic, 2015[20]).

Sweden effectively has two CSO-specific policies and also integrates civil society-related issues in other development and foreign affairs policies. The 2017 *Strategy for Support via Swedish Civil Society Organisations* (Ministry for Foreign Affairs of Sweden, 2017[21]) governs Sweden's support for framework CSOs; the Sida (2019[22]) *Guiding Principles for Sida's Engagement with and Support to Civil Society* cover all CSO and civil society support. Additionally, civil society features in the government's overarching *Policy Framework for Swedish Development Cooperation and Humanitarian Assistance* of 2016 (Government of Sweden, 2016[23]) as well as in sector strategies such as the 2018 *Strategy for Sweden's Development Cooperation in the Areas of Human Rights, Democracy and the Rule of Law* (Ministry for Foreign Affairs of Sweden, 2018[24]).

CSO survey respondents indicated that they highly value the existence of members' CSO-specific policies, as these provide a clear statement of principles and objectives to guide the member-CSO relationship. Equally, CSOs lament the absence of comprehensive CSO-specific policies. In their consultation feedback, CSOs strongly encouraged an approach of integrating civil society-related issues across a wide range of policies, inclusive of but even beyond development and foreign policy. Such an approach is seen as having the potential to advance whole-of-government coherence while being consistent with the universal nature of the 2030 Agenda commitments. Examples of policy areas that would benefit from incorporating CSO-related coverage include members' foreign policies; policies on private sector investment, trade, migration, security, taxation and digital technology; and other domestic policies or regulations directly or indirectly affecting CSOs. Incorporating the issue of civic space is seen as an important contribution to the contextual background of these policies and one that empowers policy makers to take necessary steps to address issues of civic space restrictions.

Indications are that members' policies are developed in consultation with CSOs, especially in the case of policy, strategy, principles and guidance documents. However, it is more difficult to assess whether this occurs in the case of legislation. Korea's *Policy Framework for Government-Civil Society Partnerships in International Development Cooperation* is a joint framework developed by and for the Korean development CSO umbrella network and the Korea International Cooperation Agency (Korea NGO Council for Overseas Development Cooperation and Korea International Cooperation Agency, n.d.[25]).[8] Section 2.7 discusses at greater length dialogue and consultation with CSOs in policy making.

In consultations, CSOs strongly stress the necessity of developing policy in close dialogue with CSOs, both in member and partner countries. Involving CSOs in policy development increases the likelihood that policies will reflect CSOs' experience of the member-CSO relationship and address areas of the relationship where there is room for improvement.

CSOs also stress the benefit of member collaboration with CSOs in monitoring policy implementation and in revising policy as necessary to reflect lessons gathered. Members' plans for monitoring their policies and for CSOs' involvement in such processes are not obvious from the survey findings, though this may simply be because this information is available in documents (e.g. action plans for policy implementation) that were not accessed for the survey. The 2015 Australian framework, *DFAT and NGOs: Effective Development Partners*, commits the government to collaborate with the Australian Council for International Development, the country's umbrella body of development CSOs, to monitor the policy's implementation (Department of Foreign Affairs and Trade of Australia, 2015, p. 15[26]). The 2018 AFD strategy, *Partnerships with Civil Society Organisations*, sets out annual and end-of-strategy assessments to be discussed with CSOs (French Development Agency, 2018, p. 34[27]). In accordance with *Policy for Civil Society Partnerships*, which was put in place in 2017, Global Affairs Canada (2020[28]) will engage with CSOs and their networks for annual reviews of mutual implementation.

In sum, the majority of members have policies and a handful of other members either have policies under development or consider that the integration of CSO and/or civil society issues across their development policy framework constitutes their policy. Among those members indicating that they have policies, 73% have a CSO and/or civil society-specific policy. CSOs encourage integration of civil society considerations, including that of civic space, beyond development and foreign policies to enhance coherence. The practice of consultation with CSOs in policy development is ongoing and there is more room for CSO involvement in monitoring policy implementation.

2.3. Objectives for working with CSOs and civil society

Key findings

- The majority of members identify two types of objectives for working with CSOs and civil society: first, *to reach a specific development objective (implement programmes)* and second, *to strengthen civil society in partner countries*, including supporting CSOs as independent development actors.
- Almost the same number of members select as a main objective for working with CSOs and civil society *to reach a specific development objective (implement programmes) in service delivery* as select as their main objective *to strengthen civil society in partner countries*.

As discussed in Section 1.4, members ideally would have two types of objectives for working with CSOs and civil society. One is to strengthen a pluralist and independent civil society in partner countries. The other is to meet development objectives beyond strengthening civil society in partner countries. The first type of objective is grounded in the intrinsic value of civil society and the CSOs in it. The second type of objective stems from the instrumental value placed on CSOs as a means to implement programmes targeting various other development objectives on behalf of members. USAID articulates these dual objectives well in its survey response. The agency works with CSOs as a means to help it to achieve specific development objectives other than civil society strengthening. The agency also works with CSOs as an end, recognising the intrinsic importance of a vibrant civil society sector as part of a democratic political culture and the critical role played by strong, vibrant and diverse CSOs in development.

Asked to identify their *main objective for working with CSOs and civil society*, all but three responding members select multiple main objectives.[9] As seen in survey responses (Figure 2.1), the majority of members are pursuing the two types of objectives mentioned above. The objective *to reach a specific development objective (implement programmes) linked to service delivery* is most frequently selected by members (22 responses). The objective of *strengthening civil society in partner countries, including CSOs as independent development actors* ranks a close second (21 responses). These are followed by the objective *to reach a specific development objective (implement programmes) linked to human rights and democratisation* (17 responses). The next most frequently selected objectives were *enhancing CSOs' institutional or development capacity in partner countries* and enhancing their capacity in *member countries* (16 and 12 responses respectively).

It is noteworthy that of the 22 members that indicate they work with CSOs to *reach a specific development objective (implement programmes) related to service delivery*, almost three quarters (16) also choose to work with CSOs to *strengthen civil society in partner countries*. Of the 17 that indicate they work with CSOs to *reach a specific development objective (implement programmes) related to human rights and democratisation*, almost three quarters (12) also select working with CSOs to *strengthen civil society in partner countries*.

Sections 2.3.1 through 2.3.5 highlight how members depict these varied objectives in their policy documents and survey responses. An additional objective of *public awareness raising* featured in members' survey responses and thus is also covered in this study.[10] Additionally, members' treatment of the humanitarian-development-peace nexus is briefly addressed in recognition that the nexus needs attention, especially in light of the 2019 DAC Recommendation on the Humanitarian-Development-Peace Nexus.

It is worth underlining that members' policies and objectives for working with CSOs and civil society are not static. This study presents a snapshot from late 2018 and 2019. Eleven members state that their *objectives for working with CSOs and civil society have changed in the past five years*.[11] Changes are mainly linked to new, overarching development policy directions; lessons drawn from programme implementation and evaluations; and, since 2015, emphasis on the Sustainable Development Goals (SDGs). Ireland offers an example of these shifts. The priorities set out in its 2015 policy document, *The Global Island: Ireland's Foreign Policy for a Changing World*, and in its 2013 international development policy, *One World, One Future*, have influenced Ireland's objectives for working with CSOs (Government of Ireland, 2015[29]; Government of Ireland, 2013[30]). In another example, Japan's CSO partnerships are increasingly focused on CSOs' contribution to the SDGs, as reflected in Japan's *SDGs Implementation Guiding Principles* and associated action plan (Ministry of Foreign Affairs of Japan, 2016[31]).

Figure 2.1. Member objectives for working with CSOs and civil society

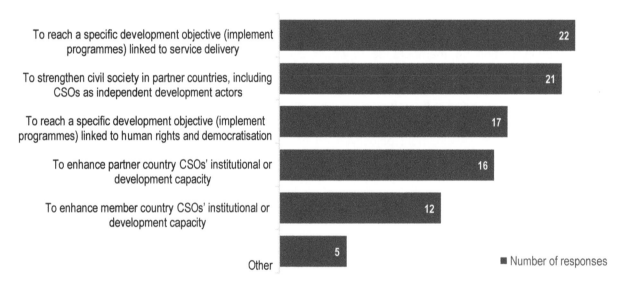

Note: A total of 29 members responded, with respondents able to select multiple options. The options shown here are shortened versions of the language used in the survey.
Source: Responses to the How DAC Members Work with Civil Society survey of members, conducted between November 2018 and March 2019.

2.3.1. Service delivery (programme implementation)

To reach a specific development objective linked to service delivery is identified by 22 members, approximately 75% of respondents, as one of their main objectives for working with CSOs and civil society. That said, member policies and narrative responses to the survey do not necessarily refer to service delivery as an objective per se. Rather, they refer to objectives such as promoting sustainable development and realising humanitarianism (Korea), reducing poverty and improving living conditions (e.g. Austrian Development Agency (ADA)), reducing inequalities (e.g. Italy), improving economic livelihoods (e.g. Australia), and protecting the planet (e.g. SDC), among others. References to CSOs as important partners in implementing the SDGs are also common.

Of course, aims such as reducing poverty or inequalities can also be achieved when members partner with CSOs to reach objectives in human rights and democratisation, or in strengthening civil society, when underlying, systemic causes of poverty and inequality can be addressed using a rights-based approach. But the prominence given to the objective of programme implementation in service delivery reflects that members' approaches to development co-operation continue to emphasise services as a way to address members' development mandates. This is evident from the figures on the volume of ODA channelled *through* CSOs by sector (Table B.4 in Annex B). Approximately 80% of such funding goes to sub-sectors such as emergency response, health, education and agriculture where service is the likely form of intervention.

Examples from member policies illustrate the varied ways in which CSOs are seen as implementing partners in service delivery. Ireland's international development policy document, *One World, One Future,* points to Irish NGOs' "pivotal role in responding to humanitarian emergencies, providing services where they are needed most, and supporting vulnerable people in developing countries to come together and participate in the development of their communities" (Government of Ireland, 2013, p. 32[30]). For the United Kingdom Department for International Development (DFID), supporting CSOs to "deliver goods, services and improvements in people's lives across DFID's work – from fragile and conflict affected states and emergency and humanitarian situations to long term development activities" is one strategy among others in the *Civil Society Partnership Review* (DFID, 2016, p. 10[32]).

Some members state that their support for CSO service provision outside of the humanitarian realm is based on the principle of subsidiarity – in other words, that CSOs have a role in complementing, but not replacing, service provision by government (e.g. ADA, Germany, Italy).

2.3.2. Human rights and democratisation (programme implementation)

The survey responses of 17 members, representing just under 60% of total respondents, identify as a main objective for their work with CSOs *to reach a specific development objective (implement programmes) linked to human rights and democratisation.*[12]

The objective for working with CSOs as implementing partners in human rights and democratisation also features in member policies and survey responses. Norad's objectives for its CSO support include democratisation and human rights, with CSOs encouraged to work towards inclusion, as well as the goal of holding governments to account for upholding human rights. Italy's development co-operation priorities include promotion of human rights, gender equality and women's empowerment and support for democracy under the rule of law. Italy's main objective for working with CSOs is to reinforce CSOs' role in contributing to the achievement of these priorities. The Luxembourg Law of 18 December 2017 articulates parameters for CSO human rights initiatives that Luxembourg will support, among them initiatives that target human rights institutions and laws, dialogue and awareness raising on rights, and the work of human rights defenders (article 4(5)) (Government of the Grand Duchy of Luxembourg, 2017[15]).

As noted, programming with CSOs in human rights and democratisation can be organised to achieve results related to reducing poverty, inequality and marginalisation, for example by addressing barriers to access to services (e.g. social accountability programming). In the consultations for this study, CSOs and members also stressed that CSO programming in service delivery can lay the groundwork for engagement in human rights and democratisation-related work. Through services, CSOs build up knowledge and understanding of the communities and partners they engage with and the legitimacy to undertake policy advocacy from a sound base of evidence and trust (Najam, 1999[33]).

2.3.3. Strengthening civil society in partner countries

Strengthening civil society in partner countries, including CSOs as independent development actors is selected as a main objective by 21 members, or almost 75% of survey respondents. Some members' policies are more explicit than others' in articulating this objective. Sida's 2019 guiding principles clearly state that supporting "a pluralistic and rights-based civil society" is "an objective in itself [given the] understanding that a strong, independent civil society is an essential part of a democratic society, and is key to inclusive and sustainable development" (Sida, 2019, p. 11[22]). The European Commission (2012, p. 4[17]), in a communication on its engagement with CSOs, stated that its support aims to contribute to the development of a dynamic, pluralistic and competent civil society. Ljungman and Nilsson (2018, p. 2[34]), evaluating Iceland's CSO support, state that its 2015 guidelines call for development support through CSOs "to contribute to an independent, strong and diverse civil society in low income countries that fights against poverty in its various forms" as the principle objective of Icelandic support for civil society. The stated purpose of Canada's *Civil Society Partnerships Policy* (paragraph 1) is to enhance effective co-operation with Canadian, international and partner country ("local") CSOs "to maximize the impact and results of Canada's international assistance and foster a strong and vibrant civil society sector", including by supporting "a robust CSO ecosystem" (Global Affairs Canada, 2020[28]). The AFD strategy, *Partnerships with Civil Society*, includes as a strategic objective the strengthening and empowering of "local civil societies" (French Development Agency, 2018, p. 6[27]).

The most commonly selected *practices used by members to strengthen civil society in partner countries* are *promoting enabling environments for CSOs and civil society in partner countries* and *providing financial support to CSOs as independent development actors in their own right* (19 responses).[13,14] Fifteen responding members require that the *member country and international CSOs they financially support work with partner country CSOs in ways that respond to the specific demands and priorities of the partner country CSOs*. Sixteen responding members *provide resources* that are not for specific CSOs but are intended to be accessible to the *civil society sector* writ large *(e.g. resource centres, training, co-ordination fora, etc.)*.

CSO survey respondents confirm that members use these methods for civil society strengthening. However, CSOs highlight barriers that hinder effective implementation, in particular the design and requirements of funding mechanisms that are less than conducive to supporting CSOs as independent development actors. CSOs also remark that members' pursuit of strengthening civil society in partner countries is haphazard when a CSO or civil society-specific policy is absent.

When it comes to one of the most frequently selected practices that can strengthen civil society in partner countries – *promoting enabling environments for CSOs and civil society in partner countries* – members use various financial and non-financial practices (Figure 2.2). The practice used by most responding members is providing *support (financial and otherwise) to CSOs and civil society, including human rights defenders, in partner countries with disenabling environments* (22 responses), closely followed by *supporting CSOs to strengthen their own effectiveness, accountability and transparency* (21 responses) and *engaging in dialogue both at the international level and with partner country governments about the need for enabling environments for CSOs* (18 responses).[15] A lesser-used practice is *self-assessment to understand and address the member's potential contribution to disenabling environments for CSOs* (7 responses). The practice used by the least number of responding members is making *financial support to partner country conditional on partner country government effort to strengthen enabling environments for CSOs and civil society* (3 responses).

Figure 2.2. Member practices to promote CSO and civil society enabling environments in partner countries

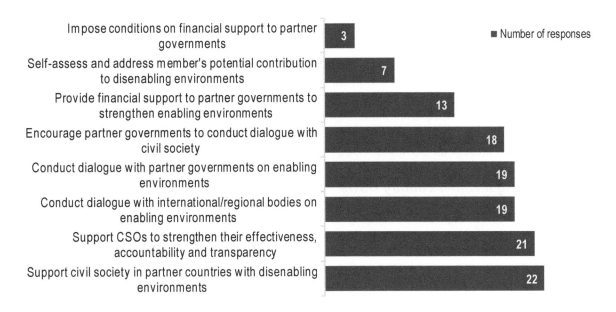

Note: A total of 24 members responded, with respondents able to select multiple options. The options shown here are shortened versions of the language used in the survey.

Source: Responses to the How DAC Members Work with Civil Society survey of members, conducted between November 2018 and March 2019.

2.3.4. Enhancing partner country CSOs' capacity

Sixteen members, approximately 55% of respondents, select *enhancing partner country CSOs' institutional or development capacity* as one of their main objectives for working with CSOs and civil society. Capacity development of partner country CSOs, most often done via member country or international CSOs, is a longstanding CSO and member practice. While members select this as a specific main objective, it is also a means of strengthening partner country civil society.

For example, an objective of Denmark's 2014 *Policy for Danish Support to Civil Society* is to "contribute to the development of a strong, independent, vocal and diverse civil society as a prerequisite to long-term poverty reduction; respect and protection of human rights; and the promotion of equality, democracy and sustainable development" (Ministry of Foreign Affairs of Denmark, 2014, p. 8[35]). The Danish policy further states that capacity development to "promote agendas for change" requires an accompanying approach in which "one civil society actor follows and guides the other through important change processes", with the organisation whose capacity is developing in the lead and owning the process (Ministry of Foreign Affairs of Denmark, 2014, pp. 8, 22[35]). In its policy, Denmark also commits to working with its CSO partners towards more systematic monitoring and reporting of capacity development processes and results.

Other members likewise refer to capacity development approaches that reflect interest in more equitable relationships between member country CSOs and their local partners. For AFD, strengthening local civil societies will happen in part through "dynamics based on enhanced reciprocity" between French and partner country CSOs (French Development Agency, 2018, pp. 6, 10[27]). In its *NGO Cooperation* policy document, Austria commits to strengthening partner country NGOs both via knowledge transfer and support from Austrian NGOs and greater transfer of responsibility and resources to partner country CSOs where conditions allow (Federal Ministry for European and International Affairs-Austrian Development

Agency, 2007, pp. 8, 10[36]). For USAID, capacity development includes support to the more traditional form of organisational development as well as to what the agency calls Capacity Development 2.0, which emphasises assisting CSOs to improve performance, strengthen networks and relationships among CSOs, and understand their role in the broader system.

Of the 13 responding members that did not select *enhancing partner country CSOs' institutional or development capacity* as a main objective, 7 selected *strengthening civil society in partner countries* as a main objective that is achieved in part through capacity development of partner country CSOs. An example is the EC, whose aim of contributing to a dynamic, pluralist and competent civil society is to be achieved through promoting a conducive environment for CSOs in partner countries, promoting participation of CSOs in partner countries' policy and increasing partner country CSOs' capacity as independent development actors (European Commission, 2012, p. 4[17]).

2.3.5. Enhancing member country CSOs' capacity

Enhancing member country CSOs' capacity is identified by 12 respondents (approximately 40% of responding members) as one of the main objectives for working with CSOs and civil society. Japan, as outlined in its *Development Cooperation Charter*, supports the development co-operation projects of Japanese NGOs and CSOs and their capacity development, with emphasis on human resources and systems development (III(2) B(e)) (Government of Japan, 2015[37]). Strengthening the technical and operational capacity of NGDOs also is an objective of Portugal's work with CSOs. Similarly, the Australian policy document, *DFAT and NGOs: Effective Development Partners*, sets out an objective of enhancing NGO performance and effectiveness that includes enhancing capabilities of Australian NGOs as development partners and building the capacity of partner country CSOs as agents of change (Department of Foreign Affairs and Trade of Australia, 2015, p. 14[26]) The Slovak Republic development co-operation strategy also notes that deployment of volunteers not only offers a form of assistance to partner countries, but builds the Slovak Republic's development co-operation capacities (Ministry of Foreign and European Affairs of the Slovak Republic, 2019, p. 26[38]).

2.3.6. Public awareness raising in member countries

It is clear from member survey responses and policy documents that the objective of public awareness raising in member countries is quite important to members. Only 2 responding members do not provide *financial support to CSOs for public awareness raising/development education/citizen engagement in development*; 17 members provide this support *as part of CSOs' development project budgets*; and 20 provide it to *specific, stand-alone public awareness/development education/citizen engagement projects by CSOs.*[16] Further, 14 members support CSOs' public awareness raising in both ways.

In its *Development Cooperation Charter*, Japan commits to encouraging the "participation of its people from all walks of life in development cooperation", including as Japan International Cooperation Agency volunteers (III(2) B(e)) (Government of Japan, 2015[37])). An objective in Australia's 2015 policy describes Australian NGOs as "a bridge between the Australian aid program and the Australian community" and thus a participant in "public diplomacy" at home (Department of Foreign Affairs and Trade of Australia, 2015, p. 10[26]). Portugal's policy, presented in *A Strategic Concept for the Portuguese Development Cooperation 2014-2020*, points to NGDOs and foundations as "key partners for debating and thinking about public policies on development, as they have in-depth knowledge of local realities and are widely recognised at local and international levels" (Government of the Portuguese Republic, 2014, p. 62[39]).

2.3.7. Humanitarian-development-peace nexus

An assessment of the state of members' efforts to address the humanitarian-development-peace nexus in relation to their work with civil society is beyond the remit of this study. Nonetheless, impressions can be gleaned from coverage in select members' civil society-related policies.[17]

The nexus is well integrated into Poland's *Multiannual Development Cooperation Programme 2016-2020*. The programme sets out Poland's two-pronged approach in its work with Polish NGOs and other actors that combines a focus on addressing urgent humanitarian needs with lasting and structural developmental measures so that these dovetail (Ministry of Foreign Affairs of Poland, 2015, pp. 10, 18, 34[12]). For other members, the need to better address the nexus is more implied than stated outright. One of the objectives of Australia's engagement with CSOs, for instance, is specific to working with CSOs to enhance their emergency response capacities while also supporting their engagement in recovery; building resilience and preparedness of communities and governments; and harnessing traditional knowledge to mitigate disaster risk (Department of Foreign Affairs and Trade of Australia, 2015, pp. 12-13[26]). As outlined in France's strategy, AFD has taken steps to better accommodate not just crisis but also post-crisis contexts and resilience through specific funding mechanisms, among them Calls for Crisis and Post-Crisis Projects, a Vulnerability Mitigation and Crisis Response Facility, and integration of the Relief-Rehabilitation-Development continuum in operations (French Development Agency, 2018, pp. 16-17[27]). These examples suggest there is growing awareness among members of the need to specifically support nexus approaches within the context of their CSO support.

In sum, almost all members indicate multiple main objectives for working with CSOs. The majority of members pursue two types of objectives: strengthening a pluralist and independent civil society in partner countries and reaching other development objectives. The most frequently selected main objective is that of working with CSOs to *reach a specific development objective (implement programmes) related to service delivery*, followed closely by the objectives to *strengthen civil society in partner countries* and to *reach a specific development objective (implement programmes) linked to human rights and democratisation*. Members give considerable importance to the objective of *public awareness raising* in member countries.

When it comes to the objective of strengthening civil society, the practice most frequently selected by members responding to the survey is *promoting enabling environments for CSOs and civil society in partner countries*. Various financial and non-financial practices are used to promote enabling environments. These range from providing support to CSOs and civil society in partner countries with disenabling environments (most frequently selected by responding members) to making members' financial support to partner countries conditional on partner country governments' efforts to strengthen enabling environments for civil society (least frequently selected by responding members).

2.4. Advantages and disadvantages of working with CSOs

Key findings

- Members identify advantages more frequently than disadvantages of working with CSOs, though both qualities are reported.
- Members identify more advantages and fewer disadvantages of working with member country or international CSOs than of working with partner country CSOs.

Many members select many advantages of working with CSOs in their survey responses. At the same time, members experience some countervailing difficulties in working with CSOs.

Among the most frequently selected *comparative advantages* of working with member country or international CSOs and with partner country CSOs are their *proximity to beneficiaries and constituencies in partner countries* and, relatedly, their *ability to reach people in vulnerable situations or facing high risk of discrimination or marginalisation* (Figure 2.3).[18,19] The ability of member country or international CSOs and partner country CSOs to *support (or provide) service delivery* in partner countries is another important comparative advantage, as is their ability to *support accountability and empowerment processes in partner countries (promote democracy)*. A smaller but still significant number of members identify these two as advantages of working with partner country CSOs.

Additional noteworthy advantages are the *specific skills and expertise* of CSOs and their ability to *quickly provide humanitarian assistance*, again with these selected by many members. Fewer members select these as advantages when the question pertains to working with partner country CSOs. The ability to provide *public awareness and engage citizens in member countries* is the most frequently selected advantage of working with member country or international CSOs.

Figure 2.3. Advantages of working with member country or international CSOs and with partner country CSOs

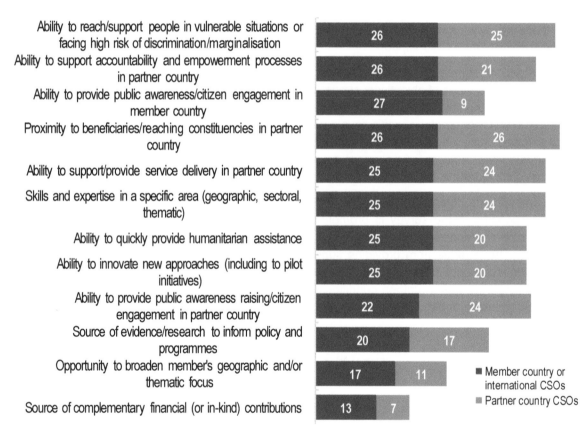

Note: A total of 29 members responded, with respondents able to select multiple options. The options shown here are shortened versions of the language used in the survey.
Source: Responses to the How DAC Members Work with Civil Society survey of members, conducted between November 2018 and March 2019.

The most frequently selected disadvantage of working with member country or international CSOs is that of *duplication and/or lack of co-ordination among CSOs*, which is also selected as a disadvantage of partner country CSOs but less frequently (Figure 2.4).[20] The most frequently selected disadvantage of working with partner country CSOs is *limitations in capacity*, which is also selected for member country or international CSOs but less frequently. The *challenge of demonstrating and aggregating development results* is attributed to working with member country or international CSOs and with partner country CSOs almost equally.

Administrative and transaction costs for the member in dealing with many small organisations are a disadvantage for just over half of responding members in regard to member country or international CSOs. A bigger share (three fifths) of responding members select this as a disadvantage of working with partner country CSOs. Many members select *legal and regulatory constraints* to financially supporting CSOs within partner countries as a disadvantage impeding work with partner country CSOs, but many also select *legal and regulatory constraints* as a disadvantage when working with member country or international CSOs. *Lack of accountability and transparency of CSOs* is identified more frequently as a disadvantage of partner country CSOs than of member country or international CSOs. Members also identify issues of *duplication and lack of co-ordination among themselves and with other donors* as a disadvantage in their work with member country or international CSOs and partner country CSOs.

Figure 2.4. Disadvantages of working with member country or international CSOs and with partner country CSOs

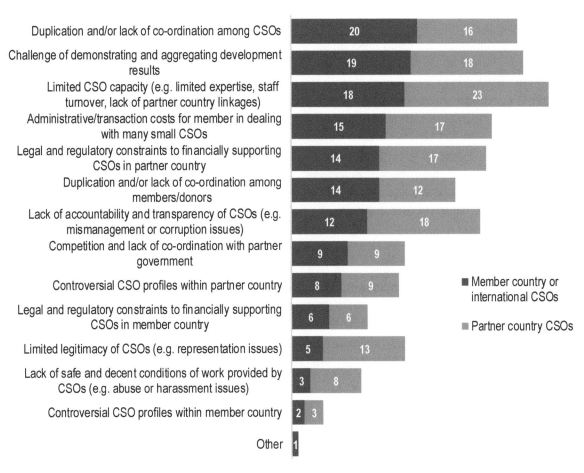

Note: A total of 29 members responded, with respondents able to select multiple options. The options shown here are shortened versions of the language used in the survey.
Source: Responses to the How DAC Members Work with Civil Society survey of members, conducted between November 2018 and March 2019.

In sum, members more frequently select advantages over disadvantages of working with CSOs. They also select more advantages and fewer disadvantages of working with member country or international CSOs than of working with partner country CSOs. Respondents select advantages of member country or international CSOs a total of 277 times, compared to 228 times in regard to partner country CSOs. They select disadvantages of member country or international CSOs 146 times, while selecting disadvantages of partner country CSOs 169 times.

Moreover, while many members appreciate CSOs for their many advantages, members are also challenged by some countervailing difficulties they experience in working with CSOs. On balance, however, an appreciation of the advantages of working with CSOs outweighs the disadvantages, with the former much more commonly identified than the latter.

2.5. How financial support is provided

Key findings

- The majority of members maintain multiple funding mechanisms to support CSOs.
- The most commonly identified mechanism of financial support for CSOs is *project/programme support*. *Partnership/framework/core support* is less common, though it is increasing incrementally.
- OECD statistics confirm members' responses, showing that most funding flows *through* CSOs as programme implementers on behalf of members and that considerably less funding flows *to* CSOs, i.e. in the form of core support to CSOs as independent development actors.
- This pattern raises a question as to whether members' financial support mechanisms adequately match their stated objectives of *reaching a specific development objective (implement programmes)* and of *strengthening civil society in partner countries, including CSOs as independent development actors*.
- Members appear to be pursuing the objective of strengthening civil society in partner countries via their *through* support.
- To better assess members' support to civil society strengthening, the data on *to* and *through* flows should be supplemented with information on the degree to which financial support mechanisms either respond to CSOs' priorities and strategies or, alternatively, rigidly steer CSOs to meet member-defined conditions (e.g. sectors, themes, countries, specific results).
- CSOs experience members' financial support mechanisms as being overly directive and steering CSOs to operate as implementers on behalf of members.

The survey finds that members tend to maintain *multiple funding mechanisms* for their CSO support.[21] Of respondents, 25 members maintain at least 2 CSO support mechanisms at *headquarters level* and only 3 have just one mechanism.[22] Additionally, 19 members maintain at least 2 CSO support mechanisms at *partner country level*, 7 have just one partner country-level mechanism and 2 have none.

Regarding financial support mechanisms managed at *headquarters level*, a majority of responding members (22) report they have *project/programme support* available *to member country CSOs*. Also regarding such mechanisms at *headquarters level*, almost half of responding members (14) report they have *partnership/framework/core support* available to *member country CSOs*. Regarding support mechanisms managed at *partner country level*, 17 responding members report they have *project/programme support available to partner country CSOs* and 16 report having *support provided via partner country governments* also available to *partner country CSOs* and to *international/regional CSOs*.

Partnership/framework/core support at *partner country level* available for *partner country CSOs* is selected by 7 members, or just under one quarter of respondents.

Within these mechanisms, members can either use a competitive process of calls for proposals or they can accept unsolicited proposals. At *headquarters level*, 24 responding members use *calls for proposals available to member country CSOs* and 16 use *calls for proposals available to international CSOs*. At *partner country level*, 15 respondents use *calls for proposals available to partner country CSOs.*

As discussed in Section 1.5, core funding mechanisms are most often used to strengthen civil society as an objective in its own right. Core support is to support CSOs to pursue their self-defined priorities while respecting CSOs' independence and right of initiative. Members also refer to partnership or framework support, which is sometimes provided as core support but can also be a hybrid of core support and project and/or programme support.[23] Project and/or programme mechanisms, on the other hand, are most often used to meet other development objectives, wherein CSOs are supported as implementing agents or instruments on behalf of members.

These survey findings indicate that mechanisms supporting CSOs as implementing partners to reach members' other development objectives are favoured over mechanisms of support to CSOs as independent development actors.

Figures from the OECD on flows from members *to* and *through* CSOs confirm that the latter type of mechanisms predominates (Figure 2.5 and Figures B.2 and B.3 in Annex B). In 2018, approximately USD 17 billion of members' bilateral ODA flowed *through* CSOs, almost six times the volume (USD 3 billion) that flowed to CSOs. In other words, 85% of members' 2018 flows for CSOs went *through* CSOs, while 15% went *to* CSOs. While the 2018 figures represent an incremental reduction in the relative share of flows *through* CSOs since 2010 (when flows *through* CSOs were almost eight times the volume of flows *to* CSOs), the dominant mechanisms are clearly channelling flows *through* CSOs.

Figure 2.5. Total ODA *to* and *through* CSOs, 2010-18, USD billion, 2018 constant prices

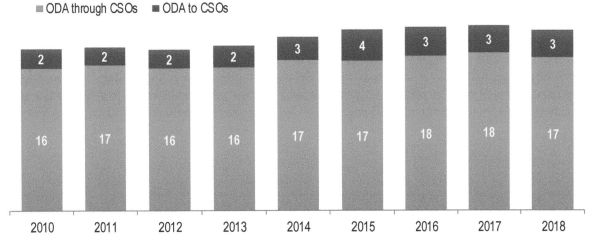

Source: (OECD, 2020[40]), *Creditor Reporting System (database)*, https://stats.oecd.org/Index.aspx?DataSetCode=crs1.

StatLink https://doi.org/10.1787/888934124299

As noted in Section 1.5, members' funding mechanisms need to match their stated objectives for working with CSOs. Given that second most frequently selected objective is *strengthening civil society in partner countries, including CSOs as independent development actors* (Figure 2.1), one would expect to see more use of partnership/framework/core support mechanisms and more flows *to* CSOs. Yet the dominant funding mechanisms and OECD statistics show that members' CSO support is predominantly channelled *through* CSOs as programme implementers to meet other, unrelated development objectives (e.g. in health, education, humanitarian assistance, etc.) on behalf of members, rather than *to* CSOs as independent development actors.

Is there thus a contradiction between stated objectives and financial support mechanisms and flows? The answer is both yes and no.

Again, as noted, OECD statistics on flows *to* and *through* CSOs do not reliably capture the volume of flows that members are allocating for one or the other of the two types of objectives. Rather, the degree to which members' financial support mechanisms tip towards being responsive to CSOs' priorities and strategies or, alternatively, rigidly steer CSOs to meet donor-defined conditions (e.g. sectors, themes, countries or even specific results) needs investigation to complement the *to* and *through* figures and the survey responses on funding mechanisms. This issue of conditional support that steers CSOs is explored in Section 1.5, which underscores the need for members' funding mechanisms to strike a balance between the conditions attached to funding on one hand and respect for CSOs as independent development actors on the other.

Member survey responses shed some light on this grey area. As noted in Section 2.3, 19 responding members consider they are *pursuing the strengthening civil society objective by supporting CSOs' right of initiative* – that is, the right of CSOs to apply for member support for initiatives in which the CSOs define their own priorities to be pursued. At the same time, 5 fewer members (14 respondents) indicate that they use core support mechanisms at *headquarters level*. Members are therefore finding ways to support CSOs' right of initiative within the framework of project and/or programme support *through* CSOs, possibly through the use of calls for proposals. In such instances, CSOs may be invited to submit proposals for self-defined initiatives, even as these initiatives must align with higher-level priorities defined by members.

Member responses to other survey questions indicate a high incidence of conditional funding that steers CSOs to meet member objectives; for some, this includes steering CSOs towards the objective of strengthening civil society in partner countries. When asked *the degree to which their financial support for CSOs must align to member-defined priority areas or themes*, almost 90% of responding members (26 responses) answer that *either all or most of their CSO support* must so align (Figure 2.6).[24] When asked if *strengthening civil society in partner countries is one of their priorities/themes*, a similar majority of responding members (25) respond positively.[25]

Figure 2.6. Member requirements for CSO support to align with member priorities

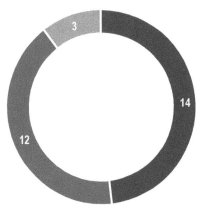

- All CSO support must align with the stated priority areas/themes
- Most CSO support must align with the stated priority areas/themes
- Only some CSO support must align with the stated priority areas/themes

Note: A total of 29 members responded. The options shown here are shortened versions of the language used in the survey.
Source: Responses to the How DAC Members Work with Civil Society survey of members, conducted between November 2018 and March 2019.

An additional consideration to help determine whether members' support mechanisms and flows *through* CSOs are conducive to meeting the strengthening civil society objective relates to support that involves capacity development. As Figure 2.1 shows, *enhancing partner country CSOs' institutional or development capacity* is also one of the main objectives for just over half (16) of responding members. In this instance, a mechanism of support *through* CSOs may be designed so that the CSOs it supports are steered to an objective of strengthening civil society in partner countries through capacity development. Further, it may be that the strengthening civil society objective is being reached in part via the considerable portion (almost 20%) of flows *through* CSOs that go to the DAC reporting directive's government and civil society sub-sector code (Table B.4 in Annex B). Though this specific sub-sector code is not limited to capturing the strengthening civil society objective, members are more likely to be reporting their support for civil society strengthening under this sub-sector than under the other, largely service delivery-oriented sub-sector options (e.g. emergency response, education, health).

Finally, the fact that members maintain multiple funding mechanisms also reinforces the idea that they are finding multiple ways to pursue the strengthening civil society objective through these varied mechanisms, including both *to* and *through* support. The Sida (2019[22]) *Guiding Principles* suggest additional ways in which this can be done. Sida provides a combination of core support *to* CSOs as independent development actors as well as support *through* CSOs to reach specific sector or thematic objectives. Capacity development and a human rights-based approach are integrated into the CSO support so that support is "for both the organizational development of the partner CSO itself, and for activities where the partner CSO develops the capacity of rights holders and accompanies them as they engage in advocacy and … improv[ing] their living conditions" (Sida, 2019, p. 11[22]). At partner country level, support *to* or *through* CSOs is pursued in co-ordination with other donors to help ensure outreach to a multitude of actors making up the civil society sector in partner countries. In addition, investments are made not only in individual CSOs but in the civil society sector as a whole. These include "public access resources", such as civil society resource centres where information and services ranging from photocopying to project management support are available, or support for networking and co-operation across civil society actors (Itad Ltd and COWI, 2012, pp. 110-111[41]; Sida, 2019, p. 12[22]).

While indications are that members are finding ways to strike a balance between steering CSOs and being responsive to them as independent development actors, responses to the survey issued to CSOs still suggest that members' financial support mechanisms fall short of an optimum balance. One CSO respondent notes that even where a member delineates principles or objectives for supporting CSOs as independent development actors, the member-CSO relationship remains "largely rooted in a transactional function, whereby CSOs are partners for the implementation of the [member] government's agenda". Another CSO respondent notes that even though a member states that it pursues the objective of enhancing CSOs as independent development actors, "the vision of CSOs just as implementing actors prevails".

CSOs also were asked whether they consider that *member mechanisms are effective and appropriate for supporting and facilitating the work of CSOs.* According to one respondent, the dominant use of project/programme support via calls for proposals is "overwhelmingly directive" and thus inconsistent with CSOs' right of initiative, while also fostering competition rather than collaboration among CSOs. Another CSO respondent sees the dominant use of project funding as a *narrow approach* that lacks flexibility and supports initiatives of too short a duration to allow for long-term capacity development of partners and, more broadly, sustainable change in partner countries. On the other hand, a CSO respondent that answered the question in the affirmative notes that the framework/partnership/core support provided has as its main objective strengthening civil society in partner countries and, beyond that, allows receiving CSOs to carry out work in keeping with their self-defined sectoral or thematic areas of focus.

Members' responses to a survey question regarding the *main influences on their decisions regarding financial support mechanisms for CSOs* (Figure 2.7) help to explain the dominance of project/programme mechanisms and *through* support. The most frequently selected influence is the *necessity of demonstrating development results* (17 responses), followed by *member government rules and regulations and/or transaction cost considerations* (12 responses) and the *influence of member country public including civil society/CSOs* (11 responses).[26]

Figure 2.7. Main influences on members' decisions regarding financial support mechanisms

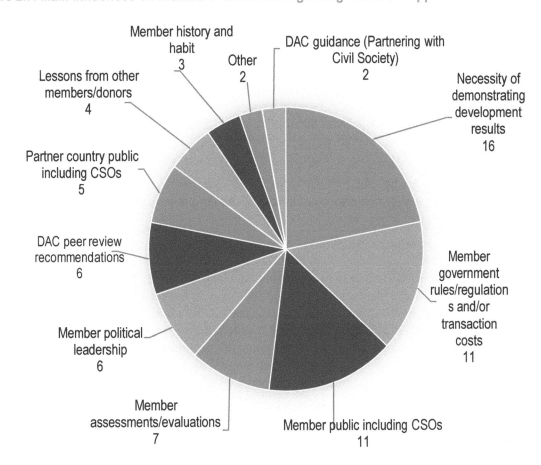

Note: A total of 21 members responded, with respondents able to select multiple options. The options shown here are shortened versions of the language used in the survey.
Source: Responses to the How DAC Members Work with Civil Society survey of members, conducted between November 2018 and March 2019.

These influences are also discussed in Section 1.5 and featured in consultations with CSOs and members. Members' results pressures incline them towards support *through* CSOs as implementing partners to meet other development objectives, especially service-oriented objectives from which tangible results are more readily demonstrated in the short term than are the results of a strengthening civil society objective. Member input from consultations suggests that such pressures are becoming even more pronounced as members tie their reporting to SDG targets. Also heard in consultations is that these pressures are felt ever more strongly in contexts of growing public and political divisions in member countries over the value of ODA.

As regards member rules and regulations and/or transaction costs considerations, members' agreement and disbursement rules and regulations can limit their ability to enter into core support arrangements, which are deemed higher risk than project/programme arrangements. In addition, a high level of due diligence assessments is required prior to providing core support and is experienced as a heavy upfront transaction cost, even though the transaction cost of core support diminishes considerably once an agreement is entered into.

That member country publics including CSO are an influencing factor for many members echoes the above-noted pressures from member publics to demonstrate development results. Moreover, domestic constituencies inclusive of CSOs have an interest in tapping into development co-operation funds and are more readily and frequently able to do so when it is in the form of project/programme funding. Consultation inputs note that core support mechanisms can be a closed shop, exclusively available to CSOs of substantial size and capacity.

In sum, findings from the survey, consultations and OECD statistics indicate that members favour mechanisms of support *through* CSOs as implementers of projects/programmes on members' behalf, and that these are more frequently used than mechanisms providing core support *to* CSOs as independent development actors. These findings suggest that members' financial support mechanisms and flows are not fully reconciled to both stated objectives for working with CSOs, i.e. to *reach a specific development objective (implement programmes)* and to *strengthen civil society in partner countries*, including CSOs as independent development actors.

In favouring project/programme support *through* CSOs, members are influenced by legal and administrative constraints and transaction cost concerns, results pressures, and the voices of member country publics and CSOs.

However, members do appear to be supporting CSOs as independent actors to some degree – and thus contributing to strengthening civil society – via their *through* support mechanisms. Supporting CSOs can take place along a spectrum ranging from more or less rigid steering of CSOs to meet member priorities to being responsive to CSOs and respecting their independence and right of initiative. Statistics on member flows *to* and *through* CSOs are too blunt an instrument to adequately assess the extent to which members are in fact pursuing the objective of strengthening civil society in partner countries, including by supporting CSOs as independent development actors. More nuanced information on the design of members' mechanisms is needed to assess the match between objectives and mechanisms of support and to evaluate what kind of balance is being struck between steering CSOs and respecting their independence.

Nonetheless, CSOs experience members' financial support mechanisms as overly directive with many conditions tied to member-defined priorities.

2.6. Who receives financial support

Key findings

- Support flows primarily for member country and international CSOs rather than for partner country CSOs, though direct member funding for partner country CSOs is increasing incrementally.
- Some members are at the early stages of seeking to work with a wider diversity of civil society actors.
- Members' rationales for favouring working with member country and international CSOs include members' rules and regulations and/or transaction cost constraints of working with partner country CSOs; longstanding and relevant experience and expertise of member country and/or international CSOs; and member country CSOs' role in public awareness raising in member countries.

2.6.1. Member country, international and partner country-based CSOs

Members' financial support flows to CSOs based in members' own countries, to international and regional CSOs, and to partner country-based CSOs. Findings from the survey of members show that all 29 responding members financially *support CSOs based in their own countries.*[27] All but one of the members responding (28) also *support international (or regional) CSOs.*

Twenty-five responding members *support partner country-based CSOs.* For the most part, members' financial support for member country and international CSOs is based on a partnership model through which these CSOs work with partner country-based CSOs (or other types of partner country-based organisations). Thus, some of the funds received by member country and international CSOs are re-allocated by these CSOs to their partner country-based CSO (or non-CSO) partners, though there is no method available at this time to confidently assess the portion of onward flows.

Unfortunately, this survey question does not distinguish between members' direct support for partner country-based CSOs and indirect support for partner country-based CSOs that flows via member country and international CSOs (or other intermediaries). However, OECD statistics show that 24 members (almost 80% of all members) provided financial support directly for developing country-based CSOs in 2018 (OECD, 2020[40]).[28] This is a slight increase over 2010, when 19 members funded partner country-based CSOs directly (OECD, 2020[40]).

Despite the high and growing number of members that, according to OECD statistics, support partner country CSOs directly, member country CSOs receive the bulk of members' financial support – approximately USD 13 billion, representing about 66% of total members flows for CSOs in 2018.

Table 2.1. ODA allocations *to* and *through* CSOs by type of CSO, 2010-18, USD billion, 2018 constant prices

Total *to* and *through*	2010	2011	2012	2013	2014	2015	2016	2017	2018
International CSO	2 885	3 447	3 587	4 032	4 221	4 601	4 934	5 266	5 459
Donor country-based CSO	13 128	13 051	12 559	12 327	13 096	14 212	14 435	14 213	13 476
Developing country-based CSO	1 048	1 157	1 263	1 490	1 478	1 403	1 283	1 404	1 417
Undefined	1 396	1 036	941	993	1 061	407	319	247	182
Aggregate	18 457	18 692	18 350	18 842	19 856	20 623	20 971	21 129	20 535

Note: The term "developing country-based" is used in this figure as it is the term used in the DAC statistical reporting directives. "Undefined" is used when member reporting does not specify the type of CSO receiving funds.
Source: (OECD, 2020[40]), *Creditor Reporting System (database)*, https://stats.oecd.org/Index.aspx?DataSetCode=crs1.

StatLink https://doi.org/10.1787/888934124356

International CSOs, the second largest recipient of member support, received approximately USD 5 billion, representing approximately 27% of flows in 2018. Developing country-based CSOs received the least amount of member funds in 2018 at approximately USD 1 billion, representing about 7% of flows in that year.[29] In 2018, members provided about ten times more support for member country CSOs than for developing country-based CSOs. This points to an incremental shift towards more direct support for partner country CSOs compared to 2010, when support was 13 times greater for member country CSOs than for developing country-based CSOs. Indeed, between 2010 and 2018, the volume of direct financial support for developing country-based CSOs increased by 35% while it increased by 3% for member country CSOs. At the same time, the support for international CSOs increased by 89% between 2010 and 2018. OECD statistics on flows for different types of CSOs are presented in Figure 2.8.

Figure 2.8. Share of ODA allocations *to* and *through* CSOs by type of CSO, 2010-18, USD billion, 2018 constant prices

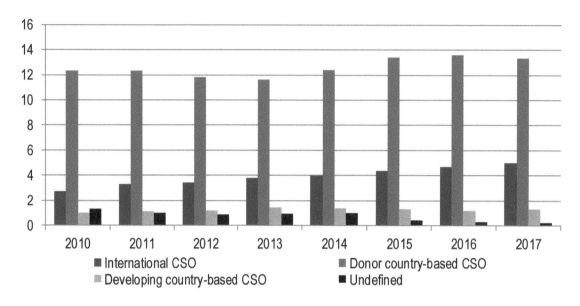

Note: The term "developing country-based" is used in this figure as it is the term used in the DAC statistical reporting directives. "Undefined" is used when member reporting does not specify the type of CSO receiving funds.
Source: (OECD, 2020[40]), *Creditor Reporting System (database)*, https://stats.oecd.org/Index.aspx?DataSetCode=crs1.

StatLink 🔗 https://doi.org/10.1787/888934124375

These shifts in the share of financial flows for member country, international and partner country CSOs are happening within a context of increasing ODA for CSOs overall. As shown in Section 1.1, member flows for CSOs increased by 11% between 2010 and 2018. Some of this increase thus seems to be directed towards partner country CSOs, as well as to international CSOs.[30]

Member survey responses and policy documents point to member efforts to channel more funds directly to partner-country based CSOs. One example is the effort of AFD, as elaborated in *Partnerships with Civil Society Organizations 2018-2023*. According to this strategy, AFD, together with the French Ministry for European and Foreign Affairs and with CSOs (via the umbrella network Coordination SUD), plans to reflect on how financing methods and conditions could be better geared for direct support for local CSOs (French Development Agency, 2018, p. 30[27]). Norway is another member that will explore ways of transferring more of its funding and decision making regarding CSO support to partner country level (Norad, 2018, p. 7[10]). Italy and Canada are seeking to provide more direct humanitarian response funding to partner country CSOs in keeping with the Grand Bargain. The EC has also tailored its funding to allow greater direct access for partner country CSOs (European Commission, 2012, p. 10[17]). According to OECD statistics, in 2018, the European Union (EU) was the top member provider of direct support for partner country CSOs, followed by the United Kingdom.

As discussed in Section 1.6, multi-donor pooled funds are a financing mechanism that members use to reach more partner country CSOs and potentially a broader swathe of civil society actors. According to member survey responses, nine responding members participate in *multi-donor pooled funds established at partner country level and accessible to partner country CSOs*.[31] Five responding members participate in such funds *established at members' headquarters level*, also *accessible to partner country CSOs*. Eight responding members also contribute to *multilateral/global funds* that are *available to partner country CSOs*, with such funds offering another way to broaden members' reach to these CSOs.

Members' survey responses indicate that south-south or triangular co-operation is another way that members seek to expand their reach to partner country-based CSOs. The member survey indicates that 11 responding members have *funding mechanisms* that *explicitly support CSOs to engage in south-south or triangular co-operation.*[32] Spain draws attention to the importance of this type of co-operation support in the more developed partner countries that Spain works with. The DFID UK Aid Connect funding mechanism supports coalitions of CSOs, think tanks, and public, private and third sector organisations, including those in partner countries, to work together to find and share innovative and flexible solutions to the most important and difficult development challenges.

Despite these various efforts, member country CSOs receive the bulk of members' CSO funding. OECD statistics show that the combined share received by member country and international CSOs amounts to 93% of members' total CSO flows. This is the case even though members find their member country CSOs (and international CSOs) and partner country CSOs fairly similarly advantaged when it comes to most of the frequently selected comparative advantages attributed to CSOs (Section 2.4, Figure 2.3).

Members' survey responses and policy documents shed some light on the pragmatic rationales for their tendency to favour working with member country CSOs. There are generally three explanations, two of which also apply to their decisions regarding international CSOs.

One rationale relates to members' legal, regulatory and administrative requirements and, relatedly, to their capacity to administer and monitor CSO support. Asked to identify the *main influences on their decisions regarding the type of CSOs supported and on their policies and strategies related to CSOs or civil society*, the largest number of responding members select *member government rules and regulations and/or transaction cost considerations* (14 responses).[33,34] Figure 2.9 shows the breakdown of responses.

Figure 2.9. Main influences on members' decisions to support particular types of CSOs and decisions on members' policies, strategies and priorities

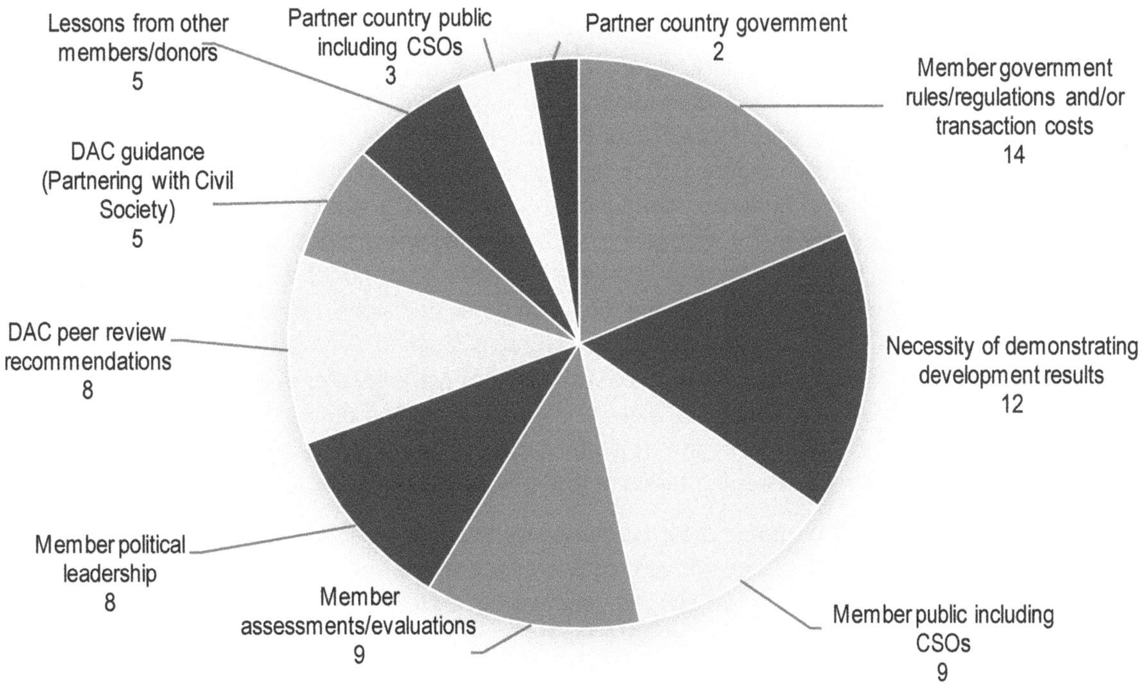

Note: A total of 22 members responded, with respondents able to select multiple options. The options shown here are shortened versions of the language used in the survey.

Source: Responses to the How DAC Members Work with Civil Society survey of members, conducted between November 2018 and March 2019.

In the case of some members (e.g. Belgium, Czech Republic, Germany, Portugal, Spain), domestic legal frameworks for development co-operation limit the type of CSO that can be directly supported.[35] Some members also note that partnering with member country (and international) CSOs is a risk management strategy, as member country legal recourse measures are more easily applied should they be needed.

Yet for other members, according to survey responses, the administrative and/or transaction cost challenge is considered a disadvantage of working with member country or international CSOs (15 responses) and with partner country CSOs (17 responses), as shown in Figure 2.4. Supporting fewer but larger and often more experienced member country or international CSOs is a way for members to manage the administrative burden that comes with direct support for a greater number of smaller and often (though not necessarily) less-experienced partner country CSOs. For example, Finland's survey response reflects the emphasis in its 2016 development policy report to the Parliament on the need for Finnish aid to support fewer and larger programmes in order to reduce the relative share of administrative work (Ministry for Foreign Affairs of Finland, 2016, p. 15[42]). Finland's primary mechanism of CSO support, which provides grants to the multi-annual programmes of experienced Finnish CSOs (and foundations), is thus considered an appropriate approach. Belgium, Iceland and Slovenia also draw attention to limited member capacity to perform due diligence and follow-up on direct partnerships with partner country CSOs. Slovenia notes that it is convenient to partner with CSOs that can work in its own language.

A second but related rationale for members to favour member country and international CSOs is the experience and expertise that these CSOs have acquired over decades of development co-operation aided by members' financial support. Member policies attest to this. The DFID *Civil Society Partnership Review* highlights the "expertise, skills and experience" of United Kingdom CSOs as "second to none" (DFID, 2016, p. 4[32]). Member country CSOs have built considerable knowledge and networks in partner countries. The Australia report, *DFAT and NGOs: Effective Development Partners*, points to the long-established connections and commitment to local communities, local networks and knowledge of international and Australian NGOs and to their trusted relationships with local actors (Department of Foreign Affairs and Trade of Australia, 2015, pp. 4-5[26]).

As discussed, members value partner country CSOs (25 responses) almost as much member country CSOs (24 responses) for their *skills and expertise in specific geographic, sectoral or thematic areas* (Figure 2.3). Additionally, *CSO capacity constraints* (including *expertise*) are identified as a disadvantage of both member country CSOs and partner country CSOs, but more so for the latter (18 versus 23 responses) (Figure 2.4). Member country CSOs are seen to have more skills, expertise and capacity, especially in meeting members' financial, administrative, monitoring and reporting requirements. The capacity of member country CSOs for monitoring and reporting results likely contributes to members' preference for working with these CSOs, given that the *necessity of demonstrating development results* is the second most frequently selected influence on members' decisions regarding the type of CSOs supported (12 responses). This is acknowledged in Norad's *Guiding Principles* for its support for civil society, which state that "[c]ivil society actors who represent or have greater access to those left behind, may lack the necessary financial or technical skills to meet Norad's and other donors' demands for direct support. Partnerships with Norwegian or international organisations, South-South partnerships, or trust fund mechanisms are a means to reaching these actors" (Norad, 2018, p. 6[10]).

A third rationale for members' preference for working with their member country CSOs stems from the value they place on public awareness raising and citizen engagement and the important role they consider that member country CSOs play. Twenty-seven responding members (93%) identified a comparative advantage of member country CSOs to be their work in *public awareness and citizen engagement* (Figure 2.3). For many members, support for CSOs is the main vehicle for increasing public awareness, support and engagement in development co-operation and global issues. Finland is a prime example, as discussed in Box 2.2. Public engagement by CSOs also provides members a way to demonstrate development results – that is, the results achieved by their CSO partners – to the public, which is an important influence on decision making. It is also worth noting that member country CSOs, on the whole, have earned the trust of member country publics thanks to their extensive experience and connections within those communities.[36]

Finland's *Guidelines for Civil Society in Development Policy* highlight the role of CSOs in promoting citizen engagement, a positive narrative around development co-operation and communication of its benefits and they refer to this role to coherently explain the advantages of working with Finnish CSOs:

"The participation of Finnish CSOs in development cooperation and humanitarian assistance adds to the Finns' understanding of and competencies in development issues. The organisations' activities in developing countries and the opportunities for participation and volunteering they provide forge contacts between Finns and the citizens of other countries. Successful communication concerning development is instrumental in that the Finns are ready to be actively involved in the promotion of global justice and burden-sharing. Understanding global problems can also reduce xenophobia and the social tensions arising from it in Finland. This is where Finnish civil society actors play an important role alongside official communications." (Ministry for Foreign Affairs of Finland, 2017, p. 12[43]).

Members also see member country CSOs as having a role in informal diplomacy. AFD deems French CSOs' participation in development co-operation "an essential driver for France's diplomacy" (French Development Agency, 2018, p. 12[27]). For DFID, a vibrant and effective civil society sector is considered part of Britain's "soft power" around the globe (DFID, 2016, p. 4[32]).

Further, just as member country CSOs are an important public engagement ally for members and a source of support for development co-operation, they also can rally political pressure domestically when their funding from members is squeezed (OECD, 2012, p. 21[44]; Wood and Fällman, 2013, p. 145[45]). Indeed, the *voice of member country CSOs and the public* is the third most frequently selected influencing factor in determining the type of CSO that members support (nine responses), which attests to member country CSOs' interest in protecting the funding they receive from members (Figure 2.9).[37]

2.6.2. Diverse civil society actors

As noted in Sections 1.2, 1.6 and 2.1, civil society is made up of diverse actors such as development or human rights CSOs, faith-based CSOs, trade unions, professional associations, social enterprises and informal associational forms, among others. Only nine members responding to the survey indicate that they support *informal associations or movements in partner countries.*[38] Five responding members indicate that *the type of CSO or civil society they support has changed in the last five years.* Some of the members that shifted support say the change is due to their increased efforts to reach to a greater diversity of CSOs and more varied associational types of civil society beyond the larger, well-established CSOs.[39]

For example, Italy has widened eligibility to allow funding of smaller CSOs that enter into partnerships and consortia with other CSOs and to allow funding of international and partner country CSOs. In 2016, the EC entered into partnership agreements with major civil society networks of NGOs, private sector organisations, trade unions, farmers' organisations, co-operatives, and community-based and faith-based organisations. Members' policy documents provide other examples. AFD, for instance, is considering opening access to actors in what it calls the "Social and Solidarity Economy" (French Development Agency, 2018, pp. 6, 29[27]). Denmark encourages its Danish and international CSO partners to work with excluded groups, informal movements and new types of civil society actors and reaches out directly to newer actors in Denmark and internationally (Ministry of Foreign Affairs of Denmark, 2014, pp. 19-20[35]). Sida is also looking into ways to broaden its support across a greater diversity of civil society actors such as social movements, digital networks and other informal associational types. As noted in Section 0, nine members participate in multi-donor pooled funds at partner country level, in part to broaden and diversify their reach across civil society.

Their own rules and regulations pose a challenge for members seeking to directly support a broader swathe of civil society, much as these stand as a challenge to direct support for partner country CSOs (see Section 0). Usually rules and regulations require that a member enter into some form of formal agreement with a legally registered organisation. USAID is one example of a member with such rules and regulations, although it is exploring mechanisms to enable support for informal groups and movements and to foster linkages between these actors and more formal CSOs.

In sum, a disproportionate share of members' funding goes for member country and international CSOs, though members' direct flows for partner country-based CSOs are increasing incrementally. While member country and international CSOs share similar advantages (and disadvantages) with partner country CSOs, members identify numerous reasons for opting to primarily support member country or international CSOs. Some members are making efforts to expand the scope of their support for a wider swathe of civil society actors, though such efforts are at an early stage.

2.7. Dialogue and consultation with CSOs and civil society

Key findings

- All members consult with CSOs regarding the member's policies, strategies or other strategic orientations.
- Regular, advance-scheduled (i.e. systematic) dialogue with CSOs is undertaken by a majority of members, especially at headquarters level with member country CSOs. Less frequent, ad hoc dialogue is undertaken with CSOs at partner country level.
- There is room for improvement in the quality and inclusivity of dialogue and consultation with CSOs and civil society at member and partner country levels.
- CSOs would welcome opportunities to participate in dialogue on member policies other than development co-operation policies.

Survey findings show that all responding members *consult with CSOs* on *member's policies, strategies, or other strategic documents* (hereinafter "policies"). As Table 2.2 illustrates, the type of policy consulted on and the type of CSO consulted vary across members. Across all types of member policies, *consultations* are mostly held with *member country CSOs*. Still, a few members engage in *consultations with partner country CSOs* across all or most of their policies. These include DFID, the EC, the Slovak Republic, the Spanish Agency for International Development Cooperation (AECID) and USAID.[40] In its survey response, USAID indicates that it consults frequently with partner CSOs at partner country level on its CSO and civil society policies during the country strategy development process and during the design phase for new activities. The AECID manual for development, monitoring and evaluation of country partnership frameworks is clear on the need to consult with stakeholders, inclusive of CSOs, in the framework country (Spanish Agency for International Development Cooperation, 2015[46]).

All responding members hold consultations with CSOs at headquarters level and 9 do not hold consultations with CSOs at partner country level.[41] Of those that hold consultations at headquarters level, 20 hold *regular, advance-scheduled* (i.e. systematic) *consultations* with CSOs at *headquarters level* and 26 hold consultations on an *as needed (ad hoc)* basis there. In addition, 7 responding members hold *regular, advance-scheduled consultations* with CSOs at *partner country level* and 20 hold *as needed (ad hoc) consultations* at *partner country level*.

Table 2.2. Types of policies consulted on and CSOs consulted with

Type of policy consulted on	Type of CSOs consulted with			
	Member country CSOs	Other member country CSOs	International or regional CSOs	Partner country CSOs
Member's policies at headquarters level	27	2	9	6
Member's policies at partner country level	19	4	11	16
Member's multilateral policies and/or strategic positions	20	2	9	5
Member's CSO and/or civil society policies at headquarters level	26	4	9	8
Member's CSO and/or civil society policies at partner country level	9	3	7	13

Note: A total of 29 members responded, with respondents able to select multiple options.
Source: Responses to the How DAC Members Work with Civil Society survey of members, conducted between November 2018 and March 2019.

Fourteen responding members state that their *approach to consultation with CSOs has changed in the last five years,* with more members undertaking systematic dialogue with CSOs.[42] The three most frequently selected *main influences* on responding members' *decisions regarding their approach to consultation with CSOs* are the *influence of the public, including CSOs, in the member country* (12 responses); *member history and habit* (10 responses); and *the necessity of demonstrating development results* tied with the *influence of member political leadership* (9 responses).[43,44]

Members' survey responses and policy documents show that they are increasingly hosting some form of platform on development co-operation in which CSOs participate alongside the member government and/or elected representatives. Platforms are diverse in their composition, set up and the scope of their subject matter. All of them include CSOs, are systematic rather than ad hoc, and address strategic and policy directions. A sampling of examples shows the diversity of member practices of dialogue and consultation with CSOs (Box 2.3).

Box 2.3. Member practices of dialogue and consultation with CSOs

Members have adopted a range of practices to include CSOs in dialogue and consultation:

- The EU Policy Forum for Development (PFD) was established in 2013 following an extensive Structured Dialogue with civil society actors and local authorities. It involves a regular cycle of global, regional and stakeholder dialogues. Governed by a jointly agreed PFD Charter, it has as objectives to facilitate dialogue on cross-cutting issues; promote policy debate and exchange of information and experiences; and support and follow up on the recommendations from the Structured Dialogue (Garcia, 2016[47]).
- Slovenia's Expert Council for Development Cooperation includes an NGO representative. In addition, its effort to include NGOs and civil society in development co-operation planning, implementation and evaluation also involves structured dialogue between the Ministry of Foreign Affairs (MFA) and the NGO Platform at least twice a year, and working exchanges between the MFA and the Platform are also encouraged (Ministry of Foreign Affairs of the Republic of Slovenia, 2013, p. 1[48]); paragraph 25 of (Government of the Republic of Slovenia, 2017[49]).
- The French National Council for Development and International Solidarity, which meets three times a year, enables dialogue between the French government and "development and international solidarity actors" inclusive of groupings of "NGOs, trade unions, employers, companies, parliamentarians, territorial authorities, universities and research institutes, and

---

high-level foreign figures" (French Development Agency, 2018, pp. 11, 15[27]). This high-level, institutionalised dialogue platform is complemented by additional strategic dialogue with CSOs on broad development co-operation policy, sector and thematic issues, and CSO funding mechanisms. Some of this is institutionalised and thus systematic; some is more informal and ad hoc.

- The NGO Working Group of the Luxembourg Ministry of Foreign and European Affairs meets at least six times a year to discuss not only policy but also CSOs' programme implementation and members' operations. Topics covered range from progress in CSOs' programmes, the status of funding opportunities and partnership agreements, plans for annual development roundtables, and even staffing changes in the ministry (Government of the Grand Duchy of Luxembourg, 2018[50]).

Members also have systematic dialogue fora on specific topics. According to its survey response, Denmark has established clusters for dialogue on specific development themes. During its 2015 evaluation of the Australian NGO Cooperation Program, the Australian Department of Foreign Affairs and Trade (DFAT) worked with the Australian Council for International Development, a network of Australian development CSOs, as a reference group to get continuous feedback on findings and recommendations (Department of Foreign Affairs and Trade of Australia and Coffey International Development, 2015, pp. iii, 24[51]). In 2018, following the launch of its *Civil Society Partnerships Policy*, Global Affairs Canada initiated a joint Advisory Group with CSOs to advise on a shared approach, vision and priorities to support the policy's implementation. Comprised of four Global Affairs Canada officials and eight CSOs selected by the civil society sector and guided by the Istanbul Principles for CSO Development Effectiveness, the advisory group is developing an implementation plan for the policy (CPAG, n.d.[52]).

Consultations with members and CSOs for this study show the value of members co-ordinating their dialogue with CSOs. Co-ordination is a way to manage consultation demands on CSOs while facilitating joint and cross-border learning. In response to a survey question on *methods used to co-ordinate and harmonise their CSO support and engagement,* members most frequently select *co-ordinated dialogues with CSOs* and *joint knowledge-sharing platforms* (15 and 10 respondents, respectively).[45]

There is minimal indication of dialogue co-ordination at partner country level. On the contrary, consultation inputs reveal instances of members creating multiple, parallel dialogue structures at partner country level. One example of co-ordinated dialogue at partner country level, however, is the development of EU Country Roadmaps for Engagement with Civil Society. The EU, with input from members and CSOs, has initiated joint analysis and planning in 107 partner countries as the basis for joint and co-ordinated programming between and among the EU and EU member states; this is sometimes co-ordinated with other donors, though the degree to which the Roadmaps are taken up by EU members to guide their strategic engagement with CSOs is said to be mixed (CONCORD, 2017, pp. 16-17[53]). At global level, the survey responses of three members (ADA, Portugal and Slovenia) cite the Global Education Network Europe in which they participate as a good practice example. The Network uses structured networking, strategy sharing and peer learning across participating members and CSOs towards improving the quality and provision of global education in Europe.

As regards *CSOs' overall level of satisfaction with members' consultation processes*, 24 of the responding members indicate that *CSOs are satisfied* with the member's consultation processes *at headquarters level*.[46],[47] Of the 20 members that hold consultations at *partner country level*, 9 indicate that *CSOs are satisfied* with the member's consultation processes.[48]

Survey responses from CSOs, however, indicate that CSOs tend to be partially rather than fully satisfied with members' consultation processes. CSOs indicate that consultation schedules do not always leave CSOs with sufficient time to prepare or ensure appropriate representation. In member countries that prioritise consultation, CSOs sometimes struggle to meet the volume of consultation demands, especially when schedules are set unilaterally by the member country government. CSOs also indicate that consultation outcomes are not necessarily relayed back to CSOs. Nor, they say, are the outcomes commensurate with the investment of time, energy and insights provided by CSOs.

According to their survey responses and consultation inputs, CSOs appreciate the existence of regular and permanent platforms for dialogue and consultation with members and would like to see more such systematic dialogues established with CSOs in partner countries. CSOs also welcome opportunities for less formal, ad hoc dialogues that allow for more frequent exchange with members on varied topics.

In consultations for this study, CSOs call for dialogue that is more inclusive of a broad swathe of civil society in both member and partner countries. They recommend that inclusivity stretch to dialogue with CSOs that are not necessarily members' direct funding partners. Transparent and clear criteria for participation would help to foster inclusivity, with the criteria informed by analysis of the civil society sector (e.g. power imbalances among CSOs, representation of the most marginalised groups, geographic spread, civic space, etc.). Inclusivity also requires that capacity challenges hindering the participation of various civil society actors, especially at partner country level, be addressed. Among the capacity challenges for CSOs are the human resources and time needed to undertake the research and analysis for well-informed engagement, as well as even the time required to travel to often centralised dialogue sites. The design of dialogue and consultation platforms also needs to account for linguistic and cultural diversity.

Survey and consultation responses from CSOs further underscore the importance of dialogue, not solely on members' development co-operation policies and strategies but also on broader subjects based on mutual interests and needs. CSOs point to the role they can play in sharing knowledge, experience and analysis drawn from their close contacts with civil society and other actors on the ground in partner countries, which can assist members to develop and implement better-informed policies and programmes in partner countries.

In sum, members are consulting more, and more systematically, on all types of policies and strategies. However, there is a greater emphasis on consultation and dialogue with member country CSOs than with partner country CSOs. This imbalance holds for co-ordination of dialogue as well. There is room for improvement in dialogue quality and inclusivity, in keeping with good practice, and dialogue on topics beyond development policy and programmes would be welcome.

2.8. Administrative requirements

Key findings

- Some members are making efforts to reduce the administrative burden of proposal, reporting and associated administrative requirements, though more could be done and by more members.
- There is minimal allowance for the use of CSOs' own proposal and reporting formats, though combined member-CSO formats are seen.
- There is a risk that new requirements from members cancel out their efforts to reduce transaction costs.
- Harmonisation of requirements across members is occurring to a limited degree, specifically through member participation in multi-donor pooled funds. The 2013 Code of Practice on Harmonisation across members could be revisited.

Survey responses and consultation inputs from members indicate a recognition that the administrative requirements of members' CSO funding tend to be burdensome, both for CSOs and members. As illustrated in Figure 2.4, approximately half of responding members identify the administrative/transaction costs of their CSO funding as a disadvantage of working with CSOs.

Survey responses point to efforts by some members to reduce the administrative burden and associated transaction costs of their CSO support. For example, the EC responds that it has introduced longer implementation periods and larger funding amounts *in the past five years*. Also notable is a new EU Financial Regulation (2018/1046) that took effect in 2018 and includes a number of simplifications and allows for further reliance on the rules and procedures of European Commission partners (European Parliament-European Council, 2018[54]).

Member survey responses and policy documents provide other examples of member efforts in this regard, including longer contracts with greater budget flexibility (ADA); simplifying and digitalising funding guidelines and procedures (AECID, Germany); accepting English as the reporting language (Czech Republic); simplifying and clarifying administrative cost coverage allowance (DFID); and reducing specific reporting requirements e.g. on public anchorage (Denmark). In Spain, a working group has been established with AEICD and the autonomous communities (regional governments) to harmonise procedures and reduce the administrative burden on CSOs. In Canada, measures to reduce the administrative burden on Global Affairs Canada and CSO partners such as simplified funding application forms and streamlined assessment processes are in place or in progress (Global Affairs Canada, 2017, p. 69[55]; Global Affairs Canada, 2020[28]). Australia's longstanding use of an accreditation process for CSO partners is reputed to streamline the due diligence process and thus reduce transaction costs for DFAT and the CSOs it funds (Department of Foreign Affairs and Trade of Australia and Coffey International Development, 2015, pp. 43-44, 59[51]).

Formats for proposal submission can be long and complex and not necessarily tailorable to CSOs' approaches or priorities. Fifteen responding members require that *funding proposal formats for CSO funding* be submitted in a *format provided by the institution*.[49] Ten responding members use formats that *combine sections pre-defined by the member with CSOs' choice of format*. Iceland, for example, requires applicants to fill out a four-page application form detailing the funding needed, timeline and project outline and to accompany this form with a more detailed proposal in a format the CSO chooses. Four responding members accept proposal submissions in a *format the CSO chooses*. Different formats can be used for different financial mechanisms. For example, when providing core support *to* CSOs, SDC has accepted proposals in CSOs' chosen format. However, for support *through* CSOs, SDC's format must be used.

CSO respondents to the CSO survey offer a mix of views regarding whether or not member proposal formats and procedures are overly burdensome on CSOs. CSOs critique members' proposal formats as demanding a level of detail that is not of clear benefit to programme planning. CSOs note that they must invest considerable time and financial resources to respond to calls for proposals, with success far from guaranteed. A positive development noted by CSOs is that members sometimes use a two-stage process involving a preliminary, less detailed concept note followed by a full proposal for partially approved candidates.

According to member survey responses, members show less flexibility on reporting formats than on proposal formats. Twenty responding members require reporting to be done in a *template provided by the member*.[50] Twelve responding members are open to *reporting that combines the member's pre-defined sections and CSOs' choice of format*.

CSO respondents to the CSO survey are again mixed in their views of whether members' reporting formats are overly burdensome or not. Those that see formats and related requirements as overly burdensome note again the high level of investment (human resources, financial) required to comply and their frustration over frequently changing formats and new requirements. In one instance, recently revised reporting formats, newly introduced requirements – for example, sign-off on integrity charters – and the obligation to report to the International Aid Transparency Initiative (IATI) standard all demand a large time investment.

As regards the *duration of members' financial support for CSOs*, 18 responding members indicate they have agreements or contracts for CSO support lasting from *one year to three years* and/or from *three years to five years*.[51] Only five respondents offer agreements and/or contracts of *more than five years* and nine offer agreements of *less than one year*. That there is a preponderance of members with agreements and/or contracts of less than five years may be due in part to inclusion of agreements for humanitarian assistance, which tend to be of shorter duration than those for development. When it comes to the *frequency for reporting for CSOs*, 19 responding members require CSOs to report *annually*, with 6 responding members requiring *bi-annual reporting* and 4 requiring *quarterly reporting*.[52]

When asked about a range of *methods* members use to *co-ordinate and harmonise their CSO support and engagement with other donors at partner country or headquarters level*, nine members select as their response *harmonising conditions for agreements and/or proposal and/or reporting requirements*.[53] Seven responding members select *joint evaluations and/or site visits* as another method to co-ordinate and harmonise their CSO support, and four responding members select the method of *joint audits*.

As seen in Sections 1.8 and 0, there is some use by members of multi-donor pooled funds, which is one way to co-ordinate and harmonise requirements. Just under one third of responding members (ten) participate in pooled funds operating at *headquarters level*, nine participate in pooled funds operating at *partner country level*, and ten contribute to *multilateral/global funds*.[54] Responding members select multiple reasons for *why* [they] *pool funding for CSOs*. The most frequently selected reason (ten) is *to enhance effective development co-operation through co-ordination and harmonisation*, the underlying rationale of which is to reduce transaction costs for fund recipients and members.[55] Other reasons for pooling funding for CSOs are, in descending order of frequency, to *find synergies and build on comparative advantages* of members (eight), *increase the funding for specific projects/programmes of CSOs* (eight), and *increase the reach and diversity of CSOs supported* (six).

More generally regarding the administrative burden of requirements placed on CSOs, survey and consultation findings give a sense that CSOs are hearing mixed messages from members. On one hand, members make official statements about reducing the administrative burden and take some steps in that regard, such as extending agreement durations or simplifying reporting formats. On the other hand, detailed rules, for instance on budget adjustments, additional reporting requirements or other due diligence requirements are felt to cancel out reductions in transaction costs. CSOs would like to see more members aligning with CSOs' own formats and requirements, rather than CSOs having to conform to the many requirements imposed by different members. They would also like to see members harmonise requirements in line with the 2013 Code of Practice on Donor Harmonisation.

Nonetheless, members make clear in consultations for this study that the requirements placed on CSOs are tied to member governments' legal, regulatory and administrative requirements and that it can be challenging to alter these requirements. Members also note that the administrative requirements of their financial support can serve to bolster CSOs' capacity by helping CSOs to better plan, monitor and manage implementation of their programmes.

In sum, members are making some effort to reduce the administrative burden associated with both the application and proposals process and the reporting by CSOs they financially support. However, members remain largely tied to traditional requirements. While they acknowledge that these can be burdensome, members also say that these requirements help them to meet their own upward accountability demands. At the same time, CSOs continue to experience the administrative and technical burden of proposals, applications and reporting to members as an ongoing hindrance to their effectiveness as development actors. More effort is needed to streamline administrative requirements while ensuring that members maintain the standards necessary to meet their domestic requirements. The 2013 Code of Practice on Harmonisation could be revisited.

2.9. Monitoring for results and learning

Key findings

- Members experience constant pressure to demonstrate results of their CSO support.
- Most members allow CSO-defined indicators to be used in results frameworks.
- There is some use of iterative or adaptive approaches to results and performance management, with an emphasis on learning to inform decision making on programme directions.

Members are under pressure to demonstrate that ODA is achieving development results. When asked to name the main influences on their decisions on policies, funding mechanisms, monitoring and reporting, and even consultations with CSOs, members consistently cite the need to demonstrate development results as one of the top three influences.

Members use various types of arrangements as the *basis for reporting and learning between the member and CSOs* (Box 2.4). Approximately half of responding members (15) use more than one type of arrangement for the different funding mechanisms they have in place.[56] Many more responding members (21) use an *agreement or contract with a results framework, for example a logical framework or results matrix with indicators* compared to the members (8) that use an *agreement or contract with objectives or milestones, but no results framework with indicators*.

Box 2.4. Basis for reporting and learning between members and CSOs

Members use a range of instruments to share reporting and learning with CSOs:

- 21 members use agreements or contracts with a results framework, for example a logical framework or a results matrix with indicators
- 16 members use agreements or contracts with (adaptive) results frameworks, for example a theory of change, logical framework or a results-matrix with indicators
- 10 members use agreements or contracts aligning to CSOs' strategic objectives and internal systems and approaches to planning, monitoring and evaluation
- 8 members use agreements or contracts with objectives or milestones, but do not use results framework with indicators.

Source: Responses to the How DAC Members Work with Civil Society survey of members, conducted between November 2018 and March 2019.

To strengthen the relevance and CSO ownership of monitoring and reporting and reduce the administrative burden on CSOs, members pursue a strategy of using indicators defined by or with CSOs in performance results frameworks or matrices. Approximately half of responding members use this type of bottom-up approach, allowing *all* (15 respondents) or *some* (16 respondents) of the *indicators in results frameworks or matrices* to be *defined by CSOs* or allowing *indicators* [to] *be jointly defined between the member and CSOs* (Box 2.5).[57] Ten responding members use more than one approach.

As one example, the format for the yearly outcome monitoring and reporting of the Belgian Federal Public Service (FPS) Foreign Affairs, Foreign Trade and Development Cooperation was developed in consultation with Belgian CSOs and combines some government-defined requirements with CSOs' defined indicators. Reporting CSOs rank their progress using a four-point scale and are not obliged to provide a detailed narrative except on objectives that receive the lowest score.

Several members refer to ways in which they are placing greater emphasis on iterative or adaptive approaches as integral to results monitoring and performance optimisation, and they note methods they are trying out to enhance learning. Just over half of responding members (16) indicate that they use *adaptive results frameworks as a basis for reporting and learning between members and CSOs* (Box 2.4).

Box 2.5. Defining results indicators

Members use indicators in a variety of ways:

- 16 members' frameworks and/or matrices for CSOs' monitoring and reporting contain both CSO-defined and member-defined indicators
- 15 members allow CSOs to define the indicators
- 9 members work with CSOs to jointly define indicators
- 2 members define the indicators for CSOs.

Source: Responses to the How DAC Members Work with Civil Society survey of members, conducted between November 2018 and March 2019).

Sida is one of the members that has embraced the iterative approach referred to as adaptive management. For Sida, adaptive management inherently recognises that development results are not always, and perhaps only rarely, achieved via a linear path. Adaptive management is a way to provide Sida staff and partners "more leeway to adjust their efforts based on their judgement and it encourages them to reconsider their strategies" (Sida, 2019[56]). Adaptive management can be an especially relevant approach when a CSO is being supported to affect transformative social or institutional changes, including strengthening civil society in partner countries, rather than when a CSO is supported as an implementing agent on behalf of a member (Sida, 2019, p. 15[22]). In another example, USAID notes in its survey response that it is increasingly using what is called a collaborating, learning and adapting (CLA) approach. Among other benefits, CLA is seen to reduce duplication through knowledge sharing and co-ordination within USAID and with other development actors; improve effectiveness by grounding programmes in evidence and proven or promising practices; and enable adaptive course corrections during implementation to shorten the path to results achievement.

Member survey responses show additional examples of member attempts to better integrate learning into monitoring processes. The use of theories of change in Belgium's five-year programmes with CSOs has encouraged more flexibility to modify programmes based on learning through implementation, while mid-term learning evaluations precede the final accountability evaluation of these programmes. Staff of the Belgium FPS Foreign Affairs organise field visits with its CSO programme partners at least once every year, and reports about these visits are published on an internal knowledge database for easy access by other staff. Irish Aid has a similar approach to country-level monitoring visits of its partners, involving both staff and a pool of consultants. A terms of reference template is used for these monitoring visits to maximise lesson learning and enrich comparative findings. In the case of ADA, CSOs themselves lead programme evaluations, but the Civil Society and Evaluation units are consulted and provide quality assurance throughout the process in a collaborative spirit that allows for joint learning while increasing the evaluations' use and quality. The Netherlands Ministry of Foreign Affairs brings together its Dialogue and Dissent partners annually to discuss results progress, implementation challenges and success strategies.

Most CSOs responding to the CSO survey, in contrast, indicate that in their experience, members are not using monitoring and reporting of CSOs' supported initiatives as a source of learning – regardless of whether the learning is by and for members, the supported CSOs or for the wider CSO community. Though monitoring reports may contain lessons learned sections, actual learning on the basis of these lessons does not appear to receive concerted attention. The responses of CSOs suggest that overall, there are missed opportunities for sharing outcomes, successes and good practices based on CSOs' lessons from monitoring.

Consultations with CSOs and members for this study reveal additional elements of good practice for monitoring and learning from results. One such element is working in a consultative, interactive way with CSO partners to develop results indicators and monitoring frameworks. Such an approach is considered a worthwhile investment in strengthening CSOs' monitoring and learning capacity, not solely for the agreement at hand but for the long term. Another necessary element of good practice is openness on the part of CSOs to report on lack of progress and openness on the part of members to accept the value of learning from failure or at least from slow progress.

Also noted in consultations is the value of including dialogue with partner country government representatives, where feasible, as part of the planning and monitoring process. This can help to foster joint learning and ensure relevance and complementarity and can be an important investment in the accountability of both CSOs and members at partner country level.

In sum, members face a dilemma when it comes to their approaches to CSOs' monitoring and reporting. They may fully understand that flexibility to use CSOs' own indicators and frameworks can increase relevance and ownership while reducing the administrative burden on CSOs. But at the same time, they are constrained by the need to demonstrate results to the public in member countries. Results monitoring is an area of ongoing effort by members to identify methods that both meet needs and better integrate learning. Iterative or adaptive approaches to results management are gaining ground.

2.10. Accountability and transparency of CSOs and members

Key findings

- A majority of members indicate that they encourage CSOs to foster relationships of accountability in the partner countries CSOs work in and that they use multiple approaches to encourage CSOs to do so.
- More members need to assess and address how they support and engage with CSOs to ensure that their practices do no harm to CSOs' accountability at partner country level.
- Members are practicing transparency by making information about their financial flows to CSOs publicly accessible, though accessibility to partner country stakeholders is inadequately addressed.

As discussed in Section 2.3.3, the practice of *supporting CSOs to strengthen their effectiveness, accountability and transparency* as a way to promote enabling environments for CSOs in partner countries is the second most frequently selected answer of responding members (Figure 2.2). Asked how they *encourage CSOs to foster relationships of accountability in the partner countries they work* in, responding members most frequently select *encouraging participatory approaches* (22 responses) (Figure 2.10).[58] The next most frequently selected options, in descending order, are *encourage co-ordination between CSOs and partner country governments and among CSOs* (19 responses) and *encouraging CSOs to adhere to reasonable regulatory requirements in partner countries* (16 responses). Fewer members indicate that they *support CSO self-regulation mechanisms in member countries/globally* (8 responses) or *in partner countries* (7 responses).[59] Additionally, 18 responding members say they encourage the use of 3 or more approaches.

Figure 2.10. Members' approaches to encourage CSOs to foster relationships of accountability in partner countries

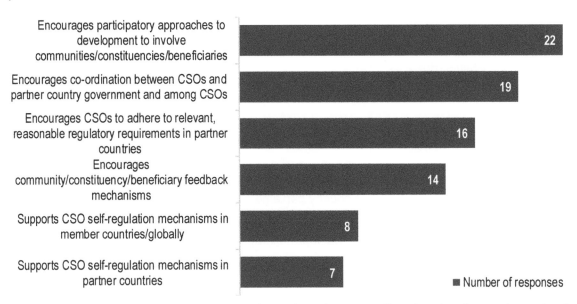

Note: A total of 23 members responded, with respondents able to select multiple options. The options shown here are shortened versions of the language used in the survey.
Source: Responses to the How DAC Members Work with Civil Society survey of members, conducted between November 2018 and March 2019.

Some members' CSO policies speak to a gamut of CSO effectiveness and accountability issues that members encourage CSOs to address. For example, for the EC, issues of CSOs' representativeness, internal governance, transparency, and co-ordination with national or local authorities are all areas of CSO responsibility that indirectly form part of the enabling environment for CSOs needing attention (European Commission, 2012, p. 6[17]). Norad's *Guiding Principles* call on CSOs to "be accountable to the affected populations" and offer examples of how to do so, including through development and implementation of publicly available ethical guidelines; whistle-blowing channels for financial irregularities, sexual harassment and other misconduct; and public disclosure of reports and evaluations, among other information (Norad, 2018, p. 8[10]).[60] Member survey responses point to member steps to promote CSOs' accountability in relation to the prevention of sexual exploitation, abuse and harassment. One example is a new financial and moral integrity charter in Belgium. Another is DFID's new safeguarding standards applied through the programme management cycle, as described in the document entitled *DFID Enhanced Due Diligence: Safeguarding for External Partners* (DFID, 2020[57]).[61]

When it comes to CSO self-regulation as an approach to encouraging CSOs to foster relationships of accountability in partner countries, three member policies encourage CSO participation in self-regulation: the EC communication entitled *The Roots of Democracy and Sustainable Development* (European Commission, 2012[17]), the Sida (2019[22]) *Guiding Principles* document, and Canada's *Policy for Civil Society Partnerships* (Global Affairs Canada, 2020[28]). In each of these, reference is made to the Istanbul Principles for CSO Development Effectiveness as an example of a CSO self-regulation initiative.

As noted (Sections 1.10 and 2.3.3), how members support and engage with CSOs has the potential to negatively affect CSOs' accountability in partner countries and can fuel the type of regulatory restrictions by partner country governments that shrink the space for CSOs' operations. Thus, the promotion of enabling environments in partner countries also requires that members self-assess to understand and address whether and how their support for and engagement with CSOs may be undermining CSOs' accountability at partner country level and, in turn, contributing to disenabling environments for civil society.

Survey responses show, however, that few members are undertaking this kind of self-assessment (Figure 2.2).

Members' own accountability at partner country level is also a concern. One way that members address their own accountability is through transparency regarding their CSO funding. According to survey responses, 18 responding members use more than one practice to *make information about their support for CSOs publicly accessible* (Box 2.6).[62]

Box 2.6. Making information about CSO support publicly accessible

The survey of members finds that:

- 15 members make annual reports available to the public
- 15 members report to their member country parliaments
- 9 members maintain an open access database covering all CSO support
- 8 members require CSOs to report to the International Aid Transparency Initiative standard
- 6 members maintain an open access database covering CSO support in specific partner countries
- 2 members provide reports to partner country governments.

Source: Responses to the How DAC Members Work with Civil Society survey of members, conducted between November 2018 and March 2019.

Responding members tend to favour practices such as *annual reports to the public* and/or to *member country parliaments* (15 responses for each option) for the purpose of making information about their CSO support publicly accessible, and 9 have established *open access databases of their CSO support*. The disadvantage of these practices, however, is that they are not necessarily disaggregated by the partner countries in which the supported CSOs operate. Nor are the partner country stakeholders necessarily aware of their existence. Few members (5) maintain or participate in *open access databases covering their CSO support in specific partner countries*. The number of members requiring CSOs to report to the IATI standard has grown in the past few years, with 8 members responding that such reporting is a requirement, although as noted, IATI data are not necessarily easily disaggregated for partner country level access either.

In sum, survey responses indicate that members recognise CSO accountability and transparency as important components of enabling environments for CSOs in partner countries. There is use among members of a mix of methods to support CSOs to enhance their accountability in partner countries. However, members have not sufficiently taken up self-assessment to better understand and address how their support and engagement with CSOs might undermine CSO accountability. At the same time, transparency regarding members' country-specific flows for CSOs is inadequately developed.

References

CONCORD (2017), *EU Delegations Report 2017: Towards a More Effective Partnership with Clvil Society*, https://concordeurope.org/wp-content/uploads/2017/03/CONCORD_EUDelegations_Report2017_EN.pdf. [53]

CPAG (n.d.), *Advisory Group to Support Implementation of the Civil Society Partnerships for International Assistance Policy: A Feminist Approach (Draft Terms of Reference)*, Ontario Council for International Cooperation, Toronto, https://www.ocic.on.ca/wp-content/uploads/2018/04/Advisory-Group-to-Support-Implementation-of-the-Civil-Society-Partnerships-for-International-Assistance-Policy.pdf. [52]

Department of Foreign Affairs and Trade of Australia (2015), *DFAT and NGOs: Effective Development Partners*, https://www.dfat.gov.au/sites/default/files/dfat-and-ngos-effective-development-partners.pdf. [26]

Department of Foreign Affairs and Trade of Australia and Coffey International Development (2015), *Evaluation of the Australian NGO Cooperation Program: Final Report*, https://dfat.gov.au/aid/how-we-measure-performance/ode/Documents/ode-evaluation-australian-ngo-cooperation-program-final-report.pdf. [51]

DFID (2020), *DFID Enhanced Due Diligence: Safeguarding for External Partners*, United Kingdom Department for International Development (DFID), London, https://www.gov.uk/government/publications/dfid-enhanced-due-diligence-safeguarding-for-external-partners/enhanced-due-diligence-safeguarding-for-external-partners. [57]

DFID (2016), *Civil Society Partnership Review*, United Kingdom Department for International Development (DFID), London, https://assets.publishing.service.gov.uk/government/uploads/system/uploads/attachment_data/file/565368/Civil-Society-Partnership-Review-3Nov2016.pdf. [32]

European Commission (2017), *The New European Consensus on Development: "Our World, Our Dignity, Our Future"*, https://op.europa.eu/en/publication-detail/-/publication/ca80bb57-6778-11e7-b2f2-01aa75ed71a1/language-en/format-PDF/source-search. [18]

European Commission (2012), "The roots of democracy and sustainable development: Europe's engagement with civil society in external relations", No. COM(2012) 492 final, https://eur-lex.europa.eu/LexUriServ/LexUriServ.do?uri=COM%3A2012%3A0492%3AFIN%3AEN%3APDF. [17]

European Parliament-European Council (2018), "Regulation (EU, Euratom) 2018/1046 on the financial rules applicable to the general budget of the Union", No. L 193/1, Official Journal of the European Union, https://eur-lex.europa.eu/legal-content/EN/TXT/PDF/?uri=CELEX:32018R1046&qid=1547825375018&from=EN. [54]

Federal Ministry for European and International Affairs-Austrian Development Agency (2007), *NGO Cooperation: Austrian Development Cooperation Policy Document*, https://www.entwicklung.at/fileadmin/user_upload/Dokumente/Publikationen/Leitlinien/Englisch/PD_NGO_Cooperation.pdf. [36]

French Development Agency (2018), *Strategy: Partnerships with Civil Society Organizations 2018-2023*, Agence Française de Développement, Paris, https://www.afd.fr/sites/afd/files/2018-07-12-05-41/CIS-AFD-OSC-VA-BD.pdf. [27]

Garcia, C. (2016), *PFD Review 2016: Executive Summary*, European Commission, Brussels, https://europa.eu/capacity4dev/policy-forum-development/document/pfd-review-2016-executive-summary-en. [47]

Global Affairs Canada (2020), *Canada's Policy for Civil Society Partnerships for International Assistance – A Feminist Approach (web page)*, https://www.international.gc.ca/world-monde/issues_development-enjeux_developpement/priorities-priorites/civil_policy-politique_civile.aspx?lang=eng. [28]

Global Affairs Canada (2017), *Canada's Feminist International Assistance Policy*, https://www.international.gc.ca/world-monde/assets/pdfs/iap2-eng.pdf?_ga=2.128420684.1524215129.1567720684-2030824443.1561580850. [55]

Government of Belgium (2016), *Arrêté royal concernant la coopération non gouvernementale [Royal Decree on non-governmental co-operation]*, http://www.ejustice.just.fgov.be/cgi_loi/change_lg.pl?language=fr&la=F&table_name=loi&cn=2016091101. [7]

Government of Belgium (2013), *Loi relative à la Coopération au Développement [Law on Development Co-operation [Law on Development Co-operation]*, http://www.ejustice.just.fgov.be/cgi_loi/change_lg.pl?language=fr&la=F&cn=2013031906&table_name=loi. [6]

Government of Ireland (2015), *The Global Island: Ireland's Foreign Policy for a Changing World*, https://www.dfa.ie/media/dfa/alldfawebsitemedia/ourrolesandpolicies/ourwork/global-island/the-global-island-irelands-foreign-policy.pdf. [29]

Government of Ireland (2013), *One World, One Future: Ireland's Policy For International Development*, http://Government of Ireland (2013), One World, One Future: Ireland's Policy For International Development, https://www.irishaid.ie/news-publications/publications/publicationsarchive/2013/may/one-world-one-future-irelands-policy/. [30]

Government of Japan (2015), *Cabinet Decision on the Development Cooperation Charter*, https://www.mofa.go.jp/files/000067701.pdf. [37]

Government of Spain (2018), *V plan director de la cooperación española 2018/2021 [Fifth Master Plan for Spanish Cooperation 2018-2021]*, http://www.exteriores.gob.es/Portal/es/SalaDePrensa/ElMinisterioInforma/Documents/V Plan Director de la Cooperación Española.pdf. [9]

Government of Spain (2014), *Ley 23/1998, de 7 de julio, de Cooperación Internacional para el Desarrollo [Law 23/1998, of July 7, on International Coooperation for Development]*, https://www.boe.es/eli/es/l/1998/07/07/23/con. [5]

Government of Sweden (2016), *Policy Framework for Swedish Development Cooperation and Humanitarian Assistance*, https://www.government.se/49a184/contentassets/43972c7f81c34d51a82e6a7502860895/skr-60-engelsk-version_web.pdf. [23]

Government of the Grand Duchy of Luxembourg (2018), *Luxembourg's General Development Cooperation Strategy: The Road to 2030*, https://cooperation.gouvernement.lu/en/publications/strategie/strategie-generale-2030.html. [16]

Government of the Grand Duchy of Luxembourg (2018), *Procès-verbal, Réunion du groupe de travail MAEE-ONG du 30 mars 2018 [Minutes of meeting of Ministry of Foreign and European Affairs-NGO working group]*, Directorate for Development Cooperation and Humanitarian Affairs, Luxembourg, https://cooperation.gouvernement.lu/dam-assets/espace-ong/groupe-de-travail-maee-ong/comptes-rendus/20180330/reunion-du-groupe-de-travail-maeemt.pdf. [50]

Government of the Grand Duchy of Luxembourg (2017), *Loi du 15 décembre 2017 modifiant la loi modifiée du 6 janvier 1996 sur la coopération au développement et l'action humanitaire [Law of 15 December 2017 modifying the Law of 6 January 1996 on development cooperation and humanitarian action]*, http://data.legilux.public.lu/file/eli-etat-leg-loi-2017-12-15-a1068-jo-fr-pdf.pdf. [15]

Government of the Grand Duchy of Luxembourg (2012), *Loi du 9 mai 2012 modifiant la loi modifiée du 6 janvier 1996 sur la coopération au développement [Law of 1 June 2012 modifying the Law of 6 January 1996 on development cooperation]*, http://data.legilux.public.lu/file/eli-etat-leg-memorial-2012-111-fr-pdf.pdf. [14]

Government of the Grandy Duchy of Luxembourg (1996), *Loi du 6 janvier 1996 sur la coopération au développement [Development Cooperation Law of 6 January 1996]*, http://legilux.public.lu/eli/etat/leg/loi/1996/01/06/n1/jo. [13]

Government of the Netherlands (2014), *Dialogue and Dissent: Strategic Partnerships for Lobbying and Advocacy*, https://www.government.nl/documents/decrees/2014/05/13/dialogue-and-dissent-strategic-partnerships-for-lobby-and-advocacy. [8]

Government of the Portuguese Republic (2014), *A Strategic Concept for the Portuguese Development Cooperation 2014-2020*, https://www.instituto-camoes.pt/images/cooperacao/160208B_ConceitoEstrategico_bilingue.pdf. [39]

Government of the Republic of Slovenia (2017), *Resolution on the International Development Cooperation and Humanitarian Aid of the Republic of Slovenia*, Government Office for Legislation, Ljubljana, http://pisrs.si/Pis.web/pregledPredpisa?id=RESO117. [49]

Itad Ltd and COWI (2012), *Support to Civil Society Engagement in Policy Dialogue: Synthesis Report*, Ministry of Foreign Affairs of Denmark, https://itad.com/wp-content/uploads/2013/02/evaluation_synthesis_report.pdf. [41]

Italian Agency for Development Cooperation (2014), *General Law on International Development Cooperation (14G00130)*, https://www.aics.gov.it/wp-content/uploads/2018/04/LEGGE_11_agosto_2014_n_125_ENGLISH.pdf. [4]

Korea NGO Council for Overseas Development Cooperation and Korea International Cooperation Agency (n.d.), *Policy Framework for Government-Civil Society Partnership in International Development Cooperation*. [25]

Ljungman, C. and A. Nilsson (2018), *Icelandic CSO Evaluation: Synthesis Report*, Government of Iceland, Reykjavík, https://www.stjornarradid.is/lisalib/getfile.aspx?itemid=c94f173e-e2a3-11e8-942d-005056bc530c. [34]

Ministry for Foreign Affairs of Finland (2017), *Guidelines for Civil Society in Development Policy*, [43]
https://um.fi/documents/35732/0/Guidelines+for+civil+society+in+development+policy.pdf/4a1
9a2aa-76fd-020e-224d-ecd98045206f.

Ministry for Foreign Affairs of Finland (2016), *Finland's Development Policy: One World, Common Future - Towards Sustainable Development*, [42]
https://um.fi/documents/35732/0/Finlands+development+policy+2016.pdf/ebf6681d-6b17-
5b27-ca88-28eae361a667?t=1561448337759.

Ministry for Foreign Affairs of Sweden (2018), *Strategy for Sweden's Development Cooperation in the Areas of Human Rights, Democracy and the Rule of Law 2018-2022*, [24]
https://www.government.se/49b9d3/contentassets/9f1870ad998f4b53a79989b90bd85f3f/rk_s
trategi-for-sveriges-utvecklingssamarbete_eng_webb22.pdf.

Ministry for Foreign Affairs of Sweden (2017), *Strategy for Support via Swedish Civil Society Organisations for the Period 2016-2022*, [21]
https://www.government.se/4a5336/contentassets/6b134cf573374ca5a247cb721c4c3456/str
ategy-for-support-via-swedish-civil-society-organisations-2016-2022.pdf.

Ministry of Foreign Affairs of Denmark (2014), *Policy for Danish Support to Civil Society*, [35]
https://amg.um.dk/policies-and-strategies/policy-for-support-to-danish-civil-society/.

Ministry of Foreign Affairs of Japan (2016), *The SDGs Implementation Guiding Principles*, [31]
https://www.mofa.go.jp/files/000252819.pdf.

Ministry of Foreign Affairs of Poland (2015), *Multiannual Development Cooperation Programme 2016-2020*, https://www.polskapomoc.gov.pl/Framework,documents,2796.html. [12]

Ministry of Foreign Affairs of the Czech Republic (2017), *Development Cooperation Strategy of the Czech Republic 2018–2030*, http://www.czechaid.cz/wp- [19]
content/uploads/2016/09/CZ_Development_Cooperation_Strategy_2018_2030.pdf.

Ministry of Foreign Affairs of the Czech Republic (2015), *Human Rights and Transition Promotion Policy Concept of the Czech Republic*, [20]
https://www.mzv.cz/file/583273/Human_rights_and_transition_promotion_policy_concept_of_t
he_Czech_Republic_.pdf.

Ministry of Foreign Affairs of the Republic of Slovenia (2013), *Guidelines on Cooperation between the Ministry of Foreign Affairs of the Republic of Slovenia, NGOs and the Network of NGOS in the Field of Development Cooperation and Humanitarian Assistance*. [48]

Ministry of Foreign and European Affairs of the Slovak Republic (2019), *Medium-term Strategy for Development Cooperation of the Slovak Republic for 2019-2023*, [38]
https://www.slovakaid.sk/sites/default/files/strednodoba_strategia_rozvojovej_spoluprace_en
g_2019-2023_644_stran_final.pdf.

Najam, A. (1999), "Citizen organizations as policy entrepreneurs", in Lewis, D. (ed.), *International Perspectives on Voluntary Action: Reshaping the Third Sector*, Earthscan, London. [33]

Norad (2018), *Norad's Support to Civil Society: Guiding Principles*, Norwegian Agency for Development Cooperation (Norad), Oslo, [10]
https://norad.no/contentassets/396cdc788c09405490a96adce80ac040/norads-support-to-
civil-society-guiding-principles.pdf.

Norwegian Ministry of Foreign Affairs (2017), *Common Responsibility for Common Future: The Sustainable Development Goals and Norway's Development Policy*, https://www.regjeringen.no/contentassets/217f38f99edf45c498befc04b7ef1f7e/en-gb/pdfs/stm201620170024000engpdfs.pdf. [11]

OECD (2020), *Creditor Reporting System (database)*, https://stats.oecd.org/Index.aspx?DataSetCode=crs1. [40]

OECD (2018), *Aid for Civil Society Organisations*, OECD, Paris, http://www.oecd.org/dac/financing-sustainable-development/development-finance-topics/Aid-for-Civil-Society-Organisations-2015-2016.pdf. [3]

OECD (2012), *Partnering with Civil Society: 12 Lessons from DAC Peer Reviews*, OECD Development Co-operation Peer Reviews, OECD Publishing, Paris, https://dx.doi.org/10.1787/9789264200173-en. [44]

OECD (2011), *How DAC Members Work with Civil Society Organisations: An Overview*, OECD Publishing, Paris, http://www.oecd.org/dac/peer-reviews/Final_How_DAC_members_work_with_CSOs_ENGLISH.pdf. [2]

OECD (2010), *Civil Society and Aid Effectiveness: Findings, Recommendations and Good Practice*, Better Aid, OECD Publishing, Paris, https://dx.doi.org/10.1787/9789264056435-en. [1]

Sida (2019), *Development cooperation with focus on adaptivity and trust (web page)*, Swedish International Development Agency (Sida), Stockholm, https://www.sida.se/English/press/current-topics-archive/2019/development-cooperation-with-focus-on-adaptivity-and-trust/. [56]

Sida (2019), *Guiding Principles for Sida's Engagement with and Support to Civil Society*, Swedish International Development Cooperation Agency (Sida), Stockholm, https://www.sida.se/contentassets/86933109610e48929d76764121b63fc6/10202931_guiding_principle_2019_no_examples_web.pdf. [22]

Spanish Agency for International Development Cooperation (2015), *Metodología Map: Manual para el Establecimiento, Seguimiento y Evaluación de los Marcos de Asociación País [Methodology Map: Manual for the Establishment, Monitoring and Evaluation of Country Partnership Frameworks]*, Agencia Española de Cooperación Internacional para el Desarrollo, Madrid, https://www.cooperacionespanola.es/sites/default/files/metodologia_map_2_cooperacion_espanola.pdf. [46]

Wood, J. and K. Fällman (2013), "Official donors' engagement with civil society: Key issues in 2012", in *State of Civil Society 2013: Creating an Enabling Environment - The Synthesis Report*, CIVICUS, Johannesburg, https://reliefweb.int/sites/reliefweb.int/files/resources/2013StateofCivilSocietyReport_full.pdf. [45]

Notes

[1] Where the exact wording or key words of a survey question are used in this chapter, they are italicised.

[2] The survey data cover 29 out of 30 members. Responses to some survey questions were mandatory; others were optional. A response to the question on how members define CSOs and civil society was optional; 22 members responded. For some of the 7 members that did not respond, policy documents contained the definitions they use or that could be inferred from the ways such documents refer to CSOs or civil society.

[3] This quotation is drawn from Belgium's survey response and the author's translation of the French version of the Belgian Law.

[4] This survey question was mandatory, and all surveyed members responded to the question.

[5] In the 2011 survey, How DAC Members Work with CSOs, only 20 members reported having a policy in place. However, the DAC had a smaller membership (24) in 2011 than in 2019, meaning that the percentage of responding members with such policies decreased from 2011 to 2019 from 87% to 76%.

[6] While Switzerland indicated in its survey response that it did not have a policy, it has since developed one and therefore is included in the 22 members with such policies.

[7] Hereinafter in this study, reference is made to policies, though the survey questions ask about members' policies/strategies.

[8] The network is the Korea NGO Council for Overseas Development Cooperation.

[9] This survey question was mandatory, and all members surveyed responded. One member, however, did not select any of the responses available for the *main objective for working with CSOs and civil society*, and instead responded with a different main objective. Members could select multiple responses.

[10] The public engagement objective was raised in several members' narrative responses to the survey. In hindsight, public engagement should have been included in the survey's list of objective options.

[11] This survey question was optional; 26 members responded to the question of whether their *objectives for working with CSOs and civil society have changed in the past five years* and 3 members did not respond.

[12] Members' selection of human rights and democratisation as an objective is complemented by the use of a human rights-based approach to development, though the two are not the same.

[13] According to the member survey, environments are considered enabling for CSOs in partner countries when legal and regulatory frameworks for the CSO sector facilitate CSOs' ability to exist and operate and when there is space for CSOs to engage in policy processes. In such environments, the rights to freedom of association, expression and peaceful assembly are respected and CSOs have access to institutionalised, multi-stakeholder spaces for dialogue where they can contribute to defining and monitoring development policy and planning.

[14] This survey question was optional; 24 members selected one or more *practices to strengthen civil society in partner countries* and 5 members did not select any. Members could select multiple responses.

[15] This survey question was optional; 24 members selected one or more *practices to promote enabling environments for CSOs and civil society in partner countries* and 5 members did not select any. Members could select multiple responses.

[16] This survey question was mandatory, and all surveyed members responded to the question.

[17] The design of the How DAC Members Work with Civil Society surveys preceded the adoption of the DAC Recommendation on the Humanitarian-Development-Peace Nexus, and coverage of the nexus was not part of the surveys. The commentary provided here on members' treatment of the Recommendation recognises that comprehensive coverage of how members are addressing the nexus is not to be found in their CSO policies. Plans for disseminating and supporting implementation and monitoring of the Recommendation are underway at the OECD Development Co-operation Directorate in collaboration with the International Network on Conflict and Fragility.

[18] This survey question asked *what does your institution identify as the comparative advantages of working with CSOs*. The question was mandatory, and all surveyed members responded to it. Members could select multiple options.

[19] There are more members that ascribe comparative advantages to member country and international CSOs than there are members that ascribe comparative advantages to partner country CSOs in all but these two comparative advantage areas. That some members do not support partner country CSOs directly does not fully explain this, as only two of the members not supporting partner country CSOs directly chose to not select any comparative advantages for partner country CSOs.

[20] This survey question was mandatory, and all surveyed members responded to it. Members could select multiple responses.

[21] While the surveys refer to *funding mechanisms/modalities*, this study refers simply to funding mechanisms.

[22] This survey question was mandatory. However, one member did not reply to this question and thus the total number of respondents is 28.

[23] For the survey, *partnership/framework* and *core support* were provided as a single option.

[24] This survey question was mandatory, and all surveyed members responded to the question.

[25] This survey question was mandatory, and all surveyed members responded to the question.

[26] This survey question was optional; 22 members selected one or more *main influences on their decisions regarding financial support mechanisms for CSOs* and 7 members did not select any. Members could select multiple responses.

[27] This survey question was mandatory, and all surveyed members responded to it. Members could select multiple responses.

[28] The term "developing country-based" is used here and elsewhere in this study specifically when referring to OECD statistics, as that is the term used in the DAC statistical reporting directives. See also Section 1.2.

[29] These percentage figures do not add up to 100% because a small portion (almost 1% in 2018) of members' CSO flows are reported in OECD statistics as undefined by CSO type.

[30] Some of the increase in the reported share of flows for developing country-based CSOs and/or for international CSOs may also be due to how flows are reported, with members now attributing to these CSOs the bulk of flows previously reported as undefined. The share of flows reported as undefined declined from almost 8% of total flows for CSOs in 2010 to almost 1% in 2018.

[31] This survey question was mandatory. However, as one member did not reply to this question, the total number of respondents is 28. Members could select multiple responses.

[32] This survey question was optional; 23 members responded to the question of whether they have *funding mechanisms* that *explicitly support CSOs to engage in south-south or triangular co-operation* and 6 did not respond to the question.

[33] This survey question was optional; 22 members selected one or more *main influences on their decisions regarding the type of CSOs supported and on their policies and strategies related to CSOs or civil society* and seven members did not select any. Members could select multiple responses.

[34] This survey question would have been more informative had it been separated into two separate queries, one on *type of CSOs supported* and a second on *policies, strategies and priorities*.

[35] It should be noted, however, that for such members, other means can be used to reach partner country-based CSOs. So while the German Federal Ministry for Economic Cooperation and Development does not directly support partner country CSOs, German implementing agencies such as Deutsche Gesellschaft für Internationale Zusammenarbeit and KfW do. The Czech Republic notes its contribution to multi-donor pooled funds and funding via the European Union and UN bodies as ways it reaches partner country-based CSOs.

[36] Of course, the level of public trust in CSOs varies by member country, by CSO and over time. Nonetheless, it can be said to be higher than public trust in partner country CSOs, as these are less directly connected to and known by member country publics.

[37] The *voice of member country CSOs and the public* tied for third place, in terms of frequency of responses, with the influence of recommendations from *members' assessments/evaluations*.

[38] This survey question was mandatory, and all surveyed members responded to the question. Members could select multiple responses.

[39] This survey question was optional; 23 members responded to the question of whether *the type of CSO or civil society they support has changed in the last five years* and 6 members did not respond to the question.

[40] Each of these members consult with partner country CSOs on at least four of the five policy areas in Table 2.2.

[41] This survey question was mandatory, and all surveyed members responded to the question. Members could select multiple responses.

[42] This survey question was optional; 24 members responded whether their *approach to consultation with CSOs has changed in the last five years* and 5 members did not respond to the question.

[43] This survey question was optional; 24 members selected one or more *main influences on their decisions regarding their approach to consultation with CSOs* and 5 members did not select any. Members could select multiple responses.

44 This survey question asked about *influences on members' decisions regarding their approach to consultation with CSOs* and members' approach *to public awareness/development education/citizen engagement.* CSOs' role in public awareness raising is discussed in Section 0.

45 This survey question was optional; 19 members selected one or more *methods used to co-ordinate and harmonise their CSO support and engagement with other donors at partner country or headquarters level* and 10 members did not select any. Members could select multiple responses.

46 This survey question was mandatory. All but one surveyed member responded, for a total of 28 respondents.

47 One member, the EC, indicates CSOs are *very satisfied* with its *consultation processes at headquarters level*; 16 members indicate that CSOs are *satisfied*; 7 indicate that CSOs are *partially satisfied;* and 5 indicate that *data on level of satisfaction is not available.* None of the responding members indicate that CSOs are *not satisfied at all* with *consultation processes at headquarters level.* One respondent indicating that *data is not available* also indicated that *CSOs are satisfied* with the consultation processes, hence the total number of responses is 29.

48 Four responding members indicate CSOs are *satisfied* with *consultation processes at partner country level* and five indicate they are *partially satisfied.* None indicate that CSOs are *very satisfied* or *not satisfied at all* with *consultation processes at partner country level.* Ten members indicate that *data on level of satisfaction is not available.*

49 This survey question was optional; 20 members selected one or more *funding proposal formats for CSO funding* and 9 members did not select any. Members could select multiple responses.

50 This survey question was mandatory. All but 2 surveyed members responded, for a total of 27 respondents. Members could select multiple responses.

51 This survey question was optional; 23 members selected one or more options related to *duration of financial support for CSOs* and six members did not select any. Members could select multiple responses.

52 This survey question was optional; 24 members selected one or more option for *frequency for reporting for CSOs* and five members did not select any. Members could select multiple responses.

53 This survey question was optional; 19 members selected one or more *methods used to co-ordinate and harmonise their CSO support and engagement with other donors at partner country or headquarters level* and 10 members did not select any. Members could select multiple responses.

54 This survey question was mandatory. However, one member did not reply to this question, thus the total number of respondents is 28. Members could select multiple responses.

55 This survey question was optional; 11 members selected one or more reasons for *why they pool funding for CSOs* and 18 members did not select any reason. Members could select multiple responses.

56 This survey question was mandatory. However, one member did not reply to this question, meaning that the total number of respondents is 28. Members could select multiple responses.

57 This survey question was mandatory. However, 2 members did not reply to this question, meaning that the total number of respondents is 27. Members could select multiple responses.

[58] This survey question was optional; 23 members selected one or more approaches to *encourage CSOs to foster relationships of accountability in the partner countries they work in* and 6 members did not select any. Members could select multiple responses.

[59] This survey question could more appropriately have asked whether members urge CSOs to *participate in* such self-regulation mechanisms rather than whether they provide *support to CSO self-regulation mechanisms*, possibly leading to a more positive responses from members.

[60] The *Guiding Principles* for Norad's support to civil society stipulate that public disclosure must be at a level of detail that does not put staff, partners or affected populations at risk.

[61] The design of the How DAC Members Work with Civil Society surveys preceded the adoption of the DAC Recommendation on Ending Sexual Exploitation, Abuse, and Harassment in Development Co-operation and Humanitarian Assistance, and coverage of the sexual exploitation, abuse and harassment issue was not part of the surveys.

[62] This survey question was optional; 24 members selected one or more practices to *make information about their CSO support publicly accessible* and 5 members did not select any. Members could select multiple responses.

3 Action points for DAC members and the OECD DAC towards enabling civil society

This chapter presents action points for members and for the OECD DAC to more effectively support and engage with civil society and civil society organisations (CSOs) and, by extension, the enabling environment for civil society. The action points are based on this study's findings from the literature, OECD statistics, survey data and inputs from consultations. They are offered to enrich and inspire further discussion among DAC members and CSOs, with a view towards developing new guidance or a recommendation to improve how members work with the civil society sector.

Members of the DAC have committed to Agenda 2030. It is clear that achieving this ambitious agenda requires all actors to engage fully and contribute their significant resources. Civil society organisations (CSOs) are valued development partners for members and are also important development actors in their own right. Virtually all members support them and engage with them and on average, 15% of members' bilateral official development assistance (ODA) flows for CSOs. Further, CSOs are a significant source of private contributions to development co-operation.

CSOs also are active players in social, economic and democratic development. They are providers of services and agents of change, drawing attention to issues that might not otherwise be addressed, channelling the voices of poor and otherwise marginalised people, and pushing for accountability from all development actors. Effective CSO support is an opportunity to facilitate CSOs' role in making sure that no one is left behind in progressing towards the Sustainable Development Goals (SDGs). This means that, crucially, members must focus on flows for CSOs and civil society.

The extensive qualitative and quantitative data gathered for this study show that members have been making changes, and continue to make changes, to their policies and objectives for working with CSOs and civil society, their financial support for CSOs, their investments in dialogue and consultation with CSOs, the administrative requirements of their CSO support, and their approaches to monitoring and learning from the CSO initiatives they support. More can be done. The literature, OECD statistics, survey data and consultation inputs collected for this study indicate ways forward to further strengthen the effectiveness of members' support for and engagement with CSOs and civil society. The concluding action points of this chapter are offered for further discussion – with DAC members and CSOs in particular, but also with the wider stakeholder community such as other providers of development co-operation, foundations and academia – and ultimately to be developed into some form of a guidance or a recommendation that builds on this study.

3.1. Action points for DAC members

3.1.1. Greater commonality is needed in member definitions of civil society and CSOs for shared understanding and to reflect civil society diversity

In focus – Action point for members

- Clarify definitions of civil society and CSOs towards a common understanding and more inclusive coverage.

The way members understand and refer to civil society and CSOs varies. For some, CSOs are understood as formal organisations within a broader civil society sector inclusive of, for example, social movements and other non-formal forms of peoples' associations. Some member definitions of or references to CSOs reflect the reality of diversity in the civil society sector and include trade unions, research and academic institutions, diaspora and migrant organisations, women's organisations, and social enterprises, among others. In other cases, members' references are to one CSO type – non-governmental organisations (NGOs) – or to non-governmental development organisations.

The diversity of the civil society sector is a challenge to establishing common definitions across members. Yet greater commonality offers clear benefits. It would foster greater coherence among members in taking up the action points from this study. It also would help CSOs, and civil society at large, to better understand which of them are the focus of particular member policies and support. Clarity in definitions of civil society and CSOs would make it easier for members to understand each other's point of reference.

The OECD and DAC definitions of CSOs (and NGOs) provide a good starting point to reach greater commonality of definitions among members. It is important, moreover, to have a broad definition of civil society and CSOs to realistically reflect the broad range of formal and informal actors that comprise the civil society sector and that fill many and varied roles in development. A broad definition is an important foundation on which members can build policies, financial support and engagement mechanisms that are inclusive and representative of the diverse civil society sector.

3.1.2. Policies for working with civil society and CSOs are needed to ensure clarity and transparency of objectives

In focus – Action points for members

- Have a civil society or CSO-specific policy document of some form (e.g. legislation, policy, strategy, principles, guidance or action plan).
- At minimum, ensure that a specific policy document addresses objectives for working with civil society and CSOs both as implementing partners and as development actors in their own right and that the document also recognises the need to strengthen a pluralist and independent civil society as an essential part of a just, democratic and sustainable society. Such a document also should address contextual issues including civic space challenges.
- Integrate CSO or civil society issues, including civic space challenges, beyond development co-operation policies and to other policy realms.
- Develop and monitor such policies in consultation with CSOs, following good practice for dialogue and consultation.

A policy document provides a transparent, overarching framework for members' support for and engagement with CSOs in development co-operation. A policy needs to provide sufficient guidance for members' decision making as regards their support and engagement with CSOs. Absent a policy, members risk that their work with CSOs is ad hoc and merely the disbursement of funds without strategic direction to meet development objectives. Currently, approximately three quarters of members indicate that they have policies for working with CSOs, with just over half of members having a CSO or civil society-specific policy.

A policy document does not have to be a policy per se, but can be in the form of legislation, a strategy, principles, guidance or an action plan. Nor does it necessarily have to be a civil society or CSO-specific document. What is important is that a key policy document spells out objectives for working with civil society and CSOs, both as members' implementing partners in development and as development actors in their own right; incorporates analysis of why the member works with civil society and CSOs; and reflects the value of CSOs as relevant and effective partners in development and the value of a diverse and independent civil society as an essential part of a just, democratic and sustainable society. The policy document should also consider contextual issues for civil society and CSOs in development including civic space challenges. In addition, a comprehensive policy would contain information on principles of working with CSOs, financial support mechanisms, a dialogue mechanism, and approaches to monitoring for results and learning. If there is a lack of certainty on some particular directions, the policy can commit to exploring options.

Members further need to integrate civil society-related issues in their broader development co-operation policies. A necessary step towards greater whole-of-government policy coherence is incorporating civil society issues, and particularly the issue of civic space, into other policy realms such as foreign policy and policies on private sector investment, trade, migration, security, taxation, digital technology and other domestic policies affecting CSOs. Such policies may not only affect CSOs' ability to contribute effectively to development. CSOs also may have valuable perspectives and experience to contribute to the development of these policies and a role to play in their implementation.

Civil society or CSO-specific policies and other policies need also to be developed and monitored in collaboration with CSOs, applying the good practices for dialogue and consultation delineated in Section 3.1.6. Without consultation, member policies will not benefit from CSOs' experience and needs and risk being irrelevant. Consultation is a necessity for transparency and to build CSO ownership of the policy directions.

3.1.3. Members should embrace two types of objectives for working with CSOs and civil society to make the most of the sector's intrinsic and instrumental value

In focus – Action points for members

- Embrace the two types of objectives for working with CSOs and civil society: one being to strengthen a pluralist and independent civil society in partner countries and the other to meet other development objectives beyond strengthening civil society in partner countries.
- Reinforce efforts to strengthen civil society in partner countries by promoting enabling environments in dialogue with partner country governments and through other methods.
- Reflect support for approaches that strengthen the humanitarian-development-peace nexus in both types of objectives.

Almost all members have multiple objectives for working with CSOs and civil society. For a majority of members, one of the main objectives is to implement programmes related to service delivery. For almost the same number of members, strengthening civil society in partner countries is also a main objective. At the level of objectives, then, a majority of members understand their CSO support as potentially two-pronged: to be a means of reaching specific development objectives other than strengthening civil society in partner countries, among them objectives related to specific sectors or themes (e.g. health, education, democratisation and gender equality), and also to contribute to reaching an objective of strong, pluralist and independent civil societies in partner countries. Members need to embrace these two types of objectives. Doing so is an important step for members to optimise their work with CSOs by recognising both the intrinsic value of civil society to a nation's social, economic and democratic development and the instrumental value of CSOs as implementing partners for members. Members must bear in mind that the risk of not embracing the objective of strengthening civil society in partner countries is that they may invest in and indeed foster CSOs and civil society that are not sufficiently locally rooted, accountable or reflective of the diversity of civil society actors in partner countries.

Members need to ensure that their policies and how they financially support and engage with CSOs reflect both types of objectives. The ways in which members provide support, the financial support mechanisms they use and the types of CSOs they support all have profound effects on CSOs and civil society sectors in partner countries and can undermine the stated objective of strengthening civil society in partner countries. Members must ensure that their working methods do no harm to CSOs and civil society in partner countries.

The most frequently identified method that members employ to strengthen civil society in partner countries is promoting enabling environments in those countries, which is critical in this era of shrinking civic space for CSOs and civil society worldwide. Members must continue to invest in this area and indeed to do more. Otherwise, members' investments can quickly be eroded as CSOs' and civil society's room to manoeuvre in partner countries becomes increasingly constrained. Members can turn to various strategies for promoting enabling environments in partner countries. Engaging in dialogue on enabling environment issues with partner country governments is one such strategy. Examples of other strategies include encouraging dialogue between CSOs and partner country governments, participating in multilateral bodies advocating for civic space, investing in partner country government institutions and enabling regulatory capacities, and engaging with private sector allies to make the business case for open civic space.

Members need also to reflect the humanitarian-development-peace nexus in their objectives for working with CSOs, with the aim of reducing people's needs, risks and vulnerabilities and preventing humanitarian crises.

3.1.4. Financial support mechanisms and flows need to reflect the two types of objectives for working with CSOs and civil society

In focus – Action points for members

- To meet both types of objectives for working with CSOs and civil society, rectify the imbalance between project/programme support mechanisms and flows *through* CSOs as programme implementers on behalf of members, on one hand, and partnership/framework/core support mechanisms and flows *to* CSOs as independent development actors, on the other.
- To help to rectify the imbalance:
  - reinforce both types of objectives within support *through* CSOs, including by minimising the degree of directiveness and designing *through* support to meet the objective of strengthening civil society in partner countries
  - increase the availability of core support *to* CSOs
  - identify ways to better demonstrate that strengthening a pluralist and independent civil society is a valuable development result
  - maintain multiple financial support mechanisms.
- Identify and rectify obstacles to supporting and incentivising more coherent humanitarian, development and peace actions in financial support mechanisms by working with CSOs to ensure that proposed solutions adequately enable them to address the nexus in their work.

Members' financial support mechanisms need to reflect their objectives for working with CSOs and civil society in terms of both how they support CSOs and which CSOs they support. However, as indicated by ODA flows *to* and *through* CSOs and the funding mechanisms members tend to prefer, members favour working with CSOs (i.e. as programme implementers on behalf of members) as a means to meet other development objectives (e.g. in health, education, democratisation and gender equality) more than working with CSOs as development actors in their own right to reach the objective of strengthening a pluralist and independent civil society. More specifically, this is suggested by the preponderance of mechanisms geared towards project/programme support (including using calls for proposals) relative to the use of partnership/framework/core support mechanisms. It is also suggested by statistics showing the bulk of members' CSO support flows *through* CSOs as programme implementers on behalf of members rather than *to* CSOs.

However, a closer look at the ways in which members design project/programme support *through* CSOs and partnership/framework/core support *to* CSOs suggests that a rigid distinction cannot be made regarding which of the two types of support is geared to meet one or both of the types of objectives. Core funding *to* CSOs is not the only means of financial support that members can provide towards the objective of strengthening civil society in partner countries. If members are constrained from providing core support

– legally, administratively or for reasons such as risk aversion or pressure to produce results, for example – they can pursue the objective of strengthening civil society in partner countries in various ways within their *through* support.

Both within and across financial support mechanisms, members primarily need to strike a better balance between rigidly steering or directing CSOs to meet member-defined conditions (e.g. sectors, themes, countries or even specific results) and being responsive to CSOs as independent development actors with their own objectives and approaches to achieving such objectives. Members must respect CSOs' right of initiative, providing them with the leeway necessary to identify programme priorities with their partner country-level constituents, partners and beneficiaries. Only half of members require that CSOs receiving funds work with their own partner country-level partners in ways that respond to the priorities and demands of these partners, and this is detrimental to achieving the member's objective of strengthening civil society in these countries. Rigid steering undermines CSOs' partner country-level accountability and credibility and creates a civil society sector that mirrors members' ever-shifting priorities but neglects other priorities.

Members can also provide support *through* CSOs that is designed specifically to meet the objective of strengthening civil society in partner countries. Since the pressure members feel to demonstrate results seems to impede the translation of this objective into mechanisms conducive to its achievement, members need to work with CSOs to better define results in terms of achieving the objective of a strengthened, pluralist and independent civil society. Results, for instance, could relate but not be limited to capacity development of individual CSOs. The type of accompaniment, enhanced reciprocity attitudes and approaches, and systems-oriented methods applied by some members are conducive to strengthening civil society and CSOs as independent development actors.

At the same time, it is clear that core support *to* CSOs is a preferred mechanism that benefits both members and CSOs. It is the type of support most suited to strengthening civil society in partner countries. Further, core funding is the most development-effective type of support, with advantages in terms of predictability, flexibility, sustainability, administrative efficiency (in the medium to long term), and, significantly, ownership and accountability. For these reasons, more financial support options in the form of core support *to* CSOs are needed from members. Core support must be given greater importance as one among multiple funding mechanisms that offer different types of support and are accessible to different types of CSOs.

In light of the 2019 DAC Recommendation on the Humanitarian-Development-Peace Nexus, members' CSO and humanitarian divisions need to work together to identify ways to better design their financial support for CSOs to support nexus approaches and to incentivise CSOs to address the nexus in their work. A coherent and co-ordinated approach is needed to members' humanitarian, development and peace investments. Otherwise, outstanding issues of vulnerability, resilience and the underlying causes of humanitarian crises will remain insufficiently addressed.

3.1.5. More financial support should be made directly available to partner country CSOs and more diverse civil society actors

In focus – Action point for members

- While sharing lessons among members and with CSOs on tackling obstacles, make additional financial support directly available to both:
  o partner country CSOs
  o and a wider swathe of civil society actors.

The bulk of members' financial support for CSOs continues to flow mainly for member country or international CSOs, though direct financial support for partner country CSOs increased incrementally in recent years. As discussed in Chapter 2, members identify many of the same comparative advantages of working with partner country CSOs and working with member country or international CSOs, which suggests that there is room to further shift the balance towards more direct support for partner country CSOs.

There are pragmatic reasons for the disproportionate investment in member country and international CSOs that will persist. These include members' legal, regulatory and administrative requirements; transaction costs and members' capacity constraints in administering and monitoring their CSO support; the extensive experience and expertise of member country and international CSOs, including in demonstrating results; and the knowledge and networks of these types of CSOs. Member country CSOs also play a critical role in public awareness and citizen engagement at home and are generally trusted by member country publics. An additional reason is the impact that member country CSOs and their domestic supporters have through their defence of members' funding allocations for these CSOs.

But these reasons should not prevent members from making additional financial support directly available to partner country CSOs and civil society. The actions points offered in this study highlight some possible steps that members can take to facilitate the provision of direct financial support, such as investing in more and better capacity development of partner country CSOs. Another step is to streamline and/or harmonise members' administrative requirements, which members can complement by allocating more human resources capacity to the management of their CSO funding.

Equally, members need to continue to explore how their support can be extended to a broader swathe of civil society actors beyond traditional development or human rights CSOs. These include forms of civil society that are often overlooked but are genuinely locally rooted and reflect what the ever-growing and diversifying civil society sector actually looks like in partner countries.

Making additional financial support available to partner country CSOs, and to that broader swathe of civil society, could help to further advance the objective of strengthening a diverse and pluralist civil society in partner countries. Absent these financial support measures, it will remain an open question whether the objective of strengthening civil society in partner countries is best met via CSOs originating from outside partner countries. Members that adopt and advance these measures can then draw out lessons from the practical steps they are taking to minimise the real and perceived obstacles – for instance, the previously discussed administrative requirements and member capacity constraints – that have led members to favour supporting member country or international CSOs. They can then share these lessons among members and with CSOs.

3.1.6. More, and more meaningful, dialogue with CSOs and civil society is needed especially at partner country level

In focus – Action points for members

- Continue to engage in systematic dialogue with member country CSOs.
- Increase systematic dialogue with CSOs in partner countries.
- Implement both systematic dialogue and ad hoc, informal dialogue.
- Encourage dialogue with CSOs beyond development and to wider foreign policy and private sector investment and trade policy.
- Encourage dialogue among CSOs and others, including partner country governments and the private sector.
- Explore co-ordination with other members for joint dialogue with CSOs.
- Implement good practice in dialogue and consultation including by addressing inclusivity, accessibility and other aspects of good practice.

Dialogue and consultation between members and CSOs are advantageous to both. Among other benefits, dialogue and consultation provide opportunities to learn from each other and ultimately to enhance the relevance and realism of members' policy and programme directions. CSOs benefit from the opportunity to engage with members on members' policies and programmes to gain insights and first-hand access to member thinking and directions. For members, dialogue with CSOs demonstrates transparency and thus is critical to ensuring their accountability to CSOs and wider publics. Dialogue is also critical to building and maintaining relationships of mutual trust and accountability between members and CSOs.

All members consult with CSOs in relation to members' policies, strategies or other strategic orientations. Members are increasingly consulting with CSOs in a systematic way through regular, advance-planned dialogue fora (i.e. institutionalised dialogue). This is much more common at headquarters level than at partner country level, however; while a majority of members still undertake consultations in partner countries, these take place on an ad hoc, as-needed basis.

Members should continue to foster dialogue and consultation with CSOs, but they need to place additional emphasis on dialogue with CSOs in partner countries. Both systematic and ad hoc dialogue are welcome. Systematic dialogue is beneficial for its predictability and transparency. Ad hoc dialogue allows members and CSOs to engage together on emerging issues, often in less formal environments that allow for open and frank discussion.

Dialogue and consultation with CSOs need also to address more than members' development policies and strategies. CSOs' experiences and their perspectives on the social, economic and political situation in partner countries are equally important. These not only can inform members' foreign policies, private sector investment and trade policies, and actions, but also can help members advance their policy coherence. Members could also foster dialogue between CSOs and other actors such as the private sector and governments in partner countries. Entry points for such dialogue include Voluntary National Reviews for the SDGs, a mechanism that all countries are meant to implement in a multi-stakeholder, consultative fashion, and the Global Partnership for Effective Development Co-operation monitoring cycle.

Members also should continue to reflect on how they undertake dialogue and consultation with CSOs so that these are meaningful and not framed as bureaucratic exercises. CSOs do not have the same staff and financial resources that members have to invest in consultations. Generous timelines for consultation are needed. Members should consider co-ordinating some of their dialogue with CSOs, especially at partner country level, as a way to help manage the consultation demands on CSOs and avoid creating parallel dialogue structures.

CSOs must be able to see that they are taken seriously, that their investments and contributions to dialogue and consultations actually have an influence on member policy and programme directions, and that their inputs are not dismissed or sidelined because they do not align with member's positions, general thinking or commonly used language. Members should focus on inclusivity, especially of marginalised groups, when designing dialogue and consultation mechanisms.

Dialogue and consultation with CSOs need to be:

- inclusive of diverse civil society actors, with particular attention to those most marginalised
- co-created with CSOs regarding both the frameworks for institutionalised dialogue and dialogue agendas
- predictable and timely, with adequate advance notice and access to documentation
- transparent throughout, such as in relation to agenda and participation criteria
- designed with feedback mechanisms on decisions made and on whether, how and why CSO inputs were used
- sufficiently resourced – including financial resources and capacity development if needed – for both the consulters and consulted
- accessible via various formats whether in person or remotely and virtually
- periodically evaluated towards ongoing improvement.

Absent attention to good practice, dialogue and consultation will appear to be nothing more than a box-ticking exercise and members will be seen as lacking accountability.

3.1.7. More effort by more members to reduce the administrative requirements of CSO support is required to lower transaction costs for members and CSOs alike

In focus – Action points for members

- Assess, seek to minimise and monitor the transaction cost burden of members' administrative requirements through:
  - o strategic, streamlined requirements
  - o use of CSOs' own or co-defined formats and systems
  - o provision of multi-year funding
  - o adaptation of requirements to contribution size and risk level
  - o co-ordination and/or harmonisation with other members, including but not limited to the use of multi-donor pooled funds.
- In addressing the transaction cost burden on CSOs, revisit the 2013 Code of Practice on Donor Harmonisation as a basis for members' individual and collective action.

CSOs and members consider members' requirements for applications, proposals and reporting overly burdensome. Moreover, there is quite an array of different requirements among members. For CSOs, and especially for those with a diversified funding base, the time, energy and other resources that they must dedicate to meeting the many requirements of different members divert them from their core business of achieving development results, whether as development actors in their own right or as programme implementers. Expending resources to meet member requirements means fewer resources are available for CSOs to invest strategically, not only in development initiatives on the ground but also in dialogue, learning, analysis, and relationships with their partners, beneficiaries and constituencies. Heavy administrative requirements also leave fewer resources available for members to address strategic issues such as expanding their reach to partner country CSOs and to a broader swathe of civil society.

Some members are making efforts to reduce the administrative burden of their CSO support. Examples include agreements of longer duration, simplified guidelines and procedures for funding applications, proposal and reporting formats that combine member-defined sections with CSOs' chosen formats, and participation in multi-donor pooled funds. On the whole, however, both members and CSOs continue to experience a heavy administrative burden, including from new requirements that quickly cancel out any transaction cost savings. Members need to make concerted efforts to streamline requirements, retaining those that are essential for due diligence and eliminating any that are extraneous. Members also should adapt requirements to the level of funding and perceived risk of the initiative and/or the CSO.

The burden of members' administrative and financial requirements is a longstanding issue in the member-CSO relationship. As members focus on easing the transaction cost burden on CSOs, they should draw on existing resources that address this issue. Specifically, it is time to revisit the 2013 Code of Practice on Donor Harmonisation and its tools, as these are as relevant, or perhaps even more relevant, today than when they were developed.

3.1.8. Further flexibility and adaptability in results monitoring, with a commitment to learning, are required for greater relevance, ownership and sustainability

In focus – Action points for members

- Work collaboratively with CSOs to define results frameworks and indicators that are most relevant to the initiative at hand and to the changes and the people the initiative is meant to address.
- Work collaboratively among members and with CSOs to explore and experiment with results indicators for civil society strengthening.
- Apply iterative approaches to results management, with greater emphasis on learning to inform programming directions in an adaptive manner.
- Invest in building the results monitoring and learning capacity of CSOs.

The pressure on members to demonstrate that ODA, including ODA for CSOs, produces development results is not expected to abate any time soon. Nor should it, given that all development co-operation stakeholders have an interest in providing the kind of results evidence that can help to maintain public and governmental support for ODA going forward. Still, the results agenda risks becoming an obsession, trumping other considerations that are known to be important in working with CSOs. To mitigate this risk, results management needs to be applied in ways that enable CSOs to still operate as independent development actors, allow them to foster local ownership and accountability at partner country levels, and embrace the non-linear, long-term change processes that many CSOs strive for.

The majority of members use traditional agreements or contracts with results frameworks. A sizable portion of members also use adaptive results frameworks as well as less linear and more context-sensitive theories of change. Members need to go further in embracing CSO-defined results and indicators to help ensure both relevance and realism in planning and monitoring and support the pursuit of results that are meaningful to partners and beneficiaries in partner countries. Otherwise, results achieved will tend to be short-term and unsustainable. Qualitative and process-oriented results indicators, including indicators that reflect the objective of strengthening civil society in partner countries, are called for. Flexibility in results management can also open opportunities for members to work with CSOs that are less experienced in results planning and monitoring. Investing in CSOs' results management capacity is worthwhile, with long-term payoffs for both CSOs and the members working with them.

Whatever results and performance management approach members use, whether the more traditional results-based management or more recent adaptive management, it is important to ensure that monitoring and reporting by CSOs and of CSOs' initiatives are done in a genuinely iterative way. Lessons drawn from results progress (or lack thereof) need to inform dialogue and decision making on the most effective directions forward, with adjustments allowed based on those learnings. Failure to take advantage of such lessons amounts to a missed opportunity, not only for improving programmes to increase the likelihood of achieving results but also for sharing successes, pitfalls and good practices based on CSOs' lessons from monitoring or otherwise.

3.1.9. Accountability and transparency of both CSOs and members need more attention, as they share responsibilities within enabling environments

In focus – Action points for members

- Integrate and support the use of a mix of methods to address CSO accountability in partner countries as central to promoting the strengthening of civil society and enabling environments.
- Recognise that members' practices of support and engagement with CSOs may, indirectly, undermine CSOs' legitimacy in partner countries and by extension weaken rather than strengthen civil society and enabling environments for civil society.
- Self-assess to ensure that members' practices of support and engagement with CSOs do no harm to CSOs' accountability in partner countries.
- Enhance transparency of funding for CSOs disaggregated by partner country and accessible to partner county stakeholders and use an appropriate level of accessibility to ensure CSOs in sensitive environments are not put at risk.

According to many members, supporting CSOs to strengthen their effectiveness, accountability and transparency is an important, albeit indirect means of promoting enabling environments for civil society in partner countries. Members need to keep this in mind and do more to promote CSO accountability at partner country level. An important action in this regard, and one that more members could take, is to urge CSOs to participate in CSO self-regulation mechanisms at partner country level. Members may also choose to invest in the establishment and operation of such mechanisms, building on lessons and the experience of various international, national and sector-level self-regulation initiatives.

Other methods that are underutilised but merit member attention include encouraging co-ordination among CSOs and between CSOs and partner country governments; instituting beneficiary and constituent feedback mechanisms; and encouraging adherence to partner country regulatory requirements. Greater investment in these methods could help mitigate the risk that members' own accountability mechanisms become a substitute for in-partner country accountability. In keeping with the DAC Recommendation on Ending Sexual Exploitation, Abuse, and Harassment in Development Co-operation and Humanitarian Assistance, members also need to invest in guiding and incentivising the CSOs they work with to develop robust internal systems to prevent and respond to sexual exploitation, abuse and harassment in their activities.

As discussed in this study, members must also reflect on whether their own methods are conducive to CSOs' pursuit of accountability towards partner country stakeholders, especially in terms of members' financial support mechanisms, the types of CSOs they support, and their administrative requirements and approaches to results monitoring. These stakeholders include beneficiaries and constituents of CSOs as well as their partners – the public and governments in partner countries. The majority of members are committed to promoting enabling environments in partner countries as one method for strengthening civil society in partner countries. Yet too few members self-assess to understand how their practices may lead, indirectly, to disenabling environments by hampering CSOs' ability to focus on their accountability relationships in partner countries.

While it is not the view of members, wider publics and partner country governments increasingly perceive CSOs as lacking the legitimacy that derives from connectedness and solidarity with local partners and beneficiaries. Members need to ensure that the way they work with CSOs no longer contributes to this perception and thus to a legitimacy and accountability crisis for CSOs. Stipulating the use of participatory methods in CSOs' programming, as many members do, is a useful but insufficient approach to promoting CSO accountability in partner countries when other aspects of members' support reorient CSOs' responsiveness and accountability squarely to meet member conditions and requirements.

Members can – and many already do – promote enabling environments in partner countries through dialogue with partner country governments and in multilateral fora, for example by encouraging and supporting dialogue spaces between CSOs and governments and through investing in partner country government institutions. But these approaches are inadequate responses to the civic space restrictions that civil society is facing. Members must also be willing to assess and address the impact of their practices of support for and engagement with CSOs and civil society. This is a question about more than whether members' practices in their work with civil society are convenient for CSOs. Their practices affect how the many CSOs that are enticed by member funding are seen in partner countries – whether or not they are considered sustainable, legitimate, grounded in and connected to local constituents and needs, or accountable at partner country level – and thus can make them vulnerable to disenabling tactics by partner country governments.

At the same time, there is ample room for members to enhance the transparency of their CSO support at partner country level, including by making information more accessible on the types of support mechanisms used and the CSOs and programmes supported. Ideally, they also would proactively ensure that partner country stakeholders know such information exists and can readily access it. On a practical level, this could mean taking steps to see that partner country stakeholders can access country-specific information of interest to them without necessarily having to search websites or global databases. In so doing, members will need to use caution to ensure that any sensitive funding flows such as to human rights defenders and CSOs in constrained environments have an appropriate level of accessibility that will not put these actors at (further) risk.

3.2. Action points for the OECD DAC

In focus – Action points for the OECD DAC

- Develop up-to-date guidance on how DAC members should work with CSOs and civil society or issue a recommendation for greater enforcement and leverage potential.
- Continue to work with the DAC Community of Practice on Civil Society to develop such a guidance or recommendation and advance its implementation by members and as a forum for peer learning.
- Tap into the dialogue opportunities with the DAC-CSO Reference Group to consult on development of the guidance or a recommendation and its implementation.
- With the Community of Practice and the DAC-CSO Reference Group, apply an iterative approach to implementation of the guidance or a recommendation with learning and ensuing adaptation embedded throughout.
- Consider, with members, revisiting OECD DAC terminology and definitions of civil society and CSOs.
- Initiate discussion with members on the usefulness and accuracy of the *to* and *through* coding of the DAC reporting directives.

One telling finding of this study is the limited influence of existing OECD DAC guidance on members' decision making regarding their work with CSOs and civil society. The 2012 OECD guidance, *Partnering with Civil Society: 12 Lessons from DAC Peer Reviews*, does not feature among the main influences most frequently selected by member survey respondents. However, recommendations from DAC peer reviews are more frequently identified as a main influence on decision making. The leading main influences cited include the need to demonstrate results, member country rules and regulations, and the influence of member country publics and CSOs.

In light of this finding, it is time for the OECD DAC to issue either clear and up-to-date guidance or a recommendation on working with CSOs and civil society. There is strong support for issuance of some form of policy instrument, whether guidance or a recommendation, within the OECD DAC and among DAC members including at leadership levels, as indicated in the 2019-20 DAC work programme and reinforced in consultations for this study. A first step is to elaborate guidance or a recommendation based on this study's findings and further consultation with members via the DAC Community of Practice on Civil Society and with CSOs via the DAC-CSO Reference Group dialogue. Another step is to continue working with the Community of Practice on Civil Society to advance implementation of such a guidance or recommendation, drawing on the Community of Practice as a forum for cross-fertilization among members, creative thinking, and sharing of lessons and ideas on how to tackle some of the most intransigent challenges in members' work with CSOs and civil society. An iterative, adaptive approach to implementation, with clear benchmarks for learning and review and in consultation with CSOs, would help to ensure relevance and realism of the policy instrument.

Also in consultation with the DAC Community of Practice and the DAC-CSO Reference Group, the OECD DAC could consider addressing some fundamental issues brought to light by this study. Among these issues are, first, the discrepancy in DAC terminology between the use of "NGO" in reporting directives and "CSO" in current literature and second, the definitions of civil society and CSO that could be updated and promoted for common usage across members.

In addition, a discussion on the usefulness and accuracy of the directives is warranted since the ways members financially support CSOs are not as clearly categorised as the DAC reporting directives' distinction between members' financial flows *to* and *through* CSOs.

Effective support for and engagement with CSOs are part and parcel of enabling environments for civil society. This study presents some of the positive trends and outstanding gaps or inconsistencies in how members work with CSOs. Its findings and proposed action points can lay the groundwork for members and CSOs to work together ever more effectively in development co-operation.

Annex A. Methodological note

The main sources of information accessed for this study are:

- a survey of DAC members and a survey of civil society organisation (CSO) networks
- literature inclusive of member policy documents, reports and evaluations, CSO studies, and academic sources
- OECD statistics on official development assistance (ODA)
- inputs from in-person and online consultations with DAC members in the Community of Practice on Civil Society and with CSOs in the DAC-CSO Reference Group and beyond.

The survey, How DAC Members Work with Civil Society, was issued to the 30 DAC members over the period of November 2018 through March 2019, and 29 members responded. Greece, while a DAC member, did not participate in the survey because it has not accepted funding proposals from CSOs since approximately 2007.

As some survey questions were optional, not all of the responses reflect the experience of all surveyed DAC members. Response rates are indicated in endnotes to the chapters.

Many DAC members maintain several funding streams for civil society and channel support from both headquarters and at partner country level. In responding to the survey questionnaire, DAC members had to generalise from these different streams.

A separate but related survey was circulated to 15 CSO networks, umbrella bodies and platforms from select member countries, partner countries, and thematic or constituency-specific CSOs. Six survey responses were received from CSO networks based in six member countries, some representing tens and others representing hundreds of members. A detailed survey of CSOs and their networks in all member countries was beyond the remit of this study. Given the millions of CSOs worldwide receiving direct or indirect support from members, the survey data can thus not be assumed to represent the civil society experience globally. However, issues raised by CSO survey respondents were echoed by CSOs in consultations for this study and in the literature, which strongly suggests that the findings of this study reflect a representative CSO experience.

Survey responses included references to the DAC member policy documents and monitoring reports that also informed this study, as well as select literature by and about CSOs and civil society in development co-operation. Chapter 2 covers the bulk of the literature reviewed. It is acknowledged that Chapter 2 does not cover all of the available literature but culls from key literature on recurring topics.

Where information has been obtained from primary sources such as member policies or evaluations, the primary source is referenced using in-text citations. Where an in-text citation is not provided, the information has been extracted from survey responses or consultation inputs.

This study uses DAC member country names except where a specific policy or practice is authored by or specifically applies to a DAC member development co-operation institution or agency, in which case the institution or agency name is used.

Annex B. DAC member financial flows for CSOs

Table B.1. Official development assistance *to* and *through* CSOs, 2010-18 (USD million, disbursements, constant 2018 prices)

	2010	2011	2012	2013	2014	2015	2016	2017	2018
Australia	379	455	480	431	498	432	335	237	263
Austria	71	61	49	70	59	55	75	100	80
Belgium	320	330	299	308	294	294	306	290	303
Canada	689	646	639	707	724	778	832	899	933
Czech Republic	0	15	15	16	16	18	20	19	23
Denmark	420	421	460	454	477	462	410	465	474
EU Institutions	1 606	1 717	1 829	1 927	2 037	1 984	2 232	2 034	2 088
Finland	178	175	174	193	200	212	129	129	121
France	147	118	136	102	246	215	223	280	339
Germany	947	902	1,019	1 066	1 112	1 160	1 437	1 581	1 610
Greece	2	0	0	0	4	0	0	0	0
Hungary	0	0	0	0	0	2	1	0	8
Iceland	0	2	3	4	3	5	7	4	6
Ireland	234	222	210	214	216	199	198	199	200
Italy	86	104	65	148	171	220	209	231	280
Japan	367	274	377	293	285	307	262	271	224
Korea	21	26	29	30	36	42	42	48	40
Luxembourg	85	79	85	88	83	81	92	92	97
Netherlands	1 497	1 355	1 214	1 212	1 136	1 164	969	962	1 032
New Zealand	46	56	47	50	55	50	52	53	54
Norway	743	731	721	800	830	874	880	900	868
Poland	0	0	0	11	14	16	16	26	27
Portugal	22	19	17	15	14	14	15	13	13
Slovak Republic	0	0	0	4	3	4	8	8	5
Slovenia	4	5	4	4	3	2	2	2	2
Spain	857	628	400	353	265	238	351	528	595
Sweden	768	836	897	941	984	994	999	1 099	1 171
Switzerland	510	528	603	666	753	849	825	815	823
United Kingdom	1 150	1 576	1 794	1 952	2 239	2 378	2 229	2 444	1 999
United States	7 306	7 412	6 786	6 784	7 098	7 575	7 815	7 403	6 841
Total	18 457	18 692	18 350	18 842	19 856	20 623	20 971	21 129	20 520

Source: (OECD, 2020[1]), *Creditor Reporting System* (database), https://stats.oecd.org/Index.aspx?DataSetCode=crs1.

Table B.2. Official development assistance *through* CSOs, 2010-18 (USD million, disbursements, constant 2018 prices)

	2010	2011	2012	2013	2014	2015	2016	2017	2018
Australia	256	293	407	286	334	293	221	231	215
Austria	70	59	49	69	58	54	73	98	79
Belgium	131	134	118	102	76	102	100	96	93
Canada	657	594	605	669	672	722	773	873	902
Czech Republic	0	15	14	15	15	17	19	18	22
Denmark	273	258	324	226	229	217	197	264	435
EU Institutions	1 606	1 717	1 827	1 924	2 029	1 975	2 221	2 022	2,068
Finland	165	163	160	178	170	176	109	105	98
France	146	117	136	101	246	200	209	258	323
Germany	947	902	1 019	1 066	1 112	455	606	753	698
Greece	2	0	0	0	4	0	0	0	0
Hungary	0	0	0	0	0	2	1	0	7
Iceland	0	0	3	3	3	5	6	3	4
Ireland	96	82	82	83	87	80	78	75	78
Italy	69	95	62	51	79	82	45	93	130
Japan	138	99	194	97	93	102	48	95	93
Korea	20	25	28	29	34	41	37	47	39
Luxembourg	63	73	77	67	64	67	60	65	79
Netherlands	1 298	1 312	1 174	1 146	1 063	1 055	849	855	938
New Zealand	26	42	32	37	39	34	36	40	44
Norway	505	489	490	545	575	604	623	636	604
Poland	0	0	0	11	14	16	15	26	27
Portugal	22	19	17	15	14	13	15	13	13
Slovak Republic	0	0	0	4	3	4	7	7	5
Slovenia	3	3	3	3	2	2	2	2	2
Spain	814	616	398	351	261	236	350	527	595
Sweden	602	712	575	612	595	538	730	863	937
Switzerland	326	350	421	459	530	609	576	552	553
United Kingdom	787	1 075	1 289	1 439	1 670	1 819	1 795	1 956	1,525
United States	7 306	7 412	6 758	6 784	7 093	7 574	7 814	7 401	6,835
Total	16 326	16 656	16 258	16 373	17 161	17 094	17 617	17 975	17,440

Source: (OECD, 2020[1]), *Creditor Reporting System* (database), https://stats.oecd.org/Index.aspx?DataSetCode=crs1.

Table B.3. Official development assistance *to* CSOs, 2010-18 (USD million, disbursements, constant 2018 prices)

	2010	2011	2012	2013	2014	2015	2016	2017	2018
Australia	123	163	73	145	165	140	115	6	48
Austria	2	1	0	2	1	1	1	1	1
Belgium	189	197	181	206	218	192	206	193	209
Canada	33	51	34	38	51	56	59	25	31
Czech Republic	0	1	1	1	1	1	1	1	1
Denmark	147	163	136	228	248	245	213	200	39
EU Institutions	0	0	3	4	8	9	11	12	21
Finland	13	12	14	15	30	36	19	24	23
France	2	1	0	2	0	15	14	22	17
Germany	0	0	0	0	0	706	831	828	913
Greece	0	0	0	0	0	0	0	0	0
Hungary	0	0	0	0	0	0	0	0	1
Iceland	0	1	0	0	0	0	0	1	2
Ireland	138	140	128	130	130	118	120	124	122
Italy	17	8	3	96	92	138	164	138	150
Japan	229	174	182	196	193	205	214	176	131
Korea	1	1	1	1	2	1	5	1	1
Luxembourg	23	7	8	21	19	14	32	27	18
Netherlands	199	43	40	65	73	109	119	107	94
New Zealand	20	14	15	13	16	15	16	13	11
Norway	238	242	231	255	255	270	257	264	264
Poland	0	0	0	0	0	0	1	0	1
Portugal	0	1	0	0	0	0	0	0	0
Slovak Republic	0	0	0	0	0	0	1	1	0
Slovenia	2	1	1	1	1	0	1	1	0
Spain	43	12	3	2	4	2	1	1	1
Sweden	166	124	322	329	389	456	269	236	234
Switzerland	184	178	182	207	223	240	249	262	270
United Kingdom	363	501	505	513	569	559	433	487	474
United States	0	0	28	0	5	1	2	2	5
Total	2 131	2 036	2 091	2 469	2 695	3 529	3 355	3 154	3 080

Source: (OECD, 2020[1]), *Creditor Reporting System* (database), https://stats.oecd.org/Index.aspx?DataSetCode=crs1.

Table B.4. Volume of official development assistance *through* CSOs by sector, 2010-18 (USD million, disbursements, constant 2018 prices)

DAC Sector	2010	2011	2012	2013	2014	2015	2016	2017	2018
Social infrastructure & services	**8 661**	**8 805**	**9 597**	**9 420**	**9 430**	**8 588**	**8 714**	**8 442**	**8 311**
Education	925	862	938	803	766	835	1 064	1 029	962
Health	989	1 190	1 245	1 376	1 557	1 458	1 349	1 131	1 051
Population Policies & Reproductive Health	2 656	2 791	2 909	2 926	2 704	2 562	2 612	2 400	2 130
Water Supply & Sanitation	330	322	356	342	401	429	356	360	346
Government & Civil Society	3 092	3 048	3 614	3 475	3 495	2 946	2 988	3 155	3 409
'- Of Which support to women's equality organisations	*182*	*283*	*204*	*150*	*169*	*276*	*210*	*163*	*251*
Social Infrastructures & Services	669	591	535	499	506	358	345	367	414
Economic infrastructure & services	**591**	**546**	**443**	**515**	**462**	**367**	**434**	**416**	**438**
Transport & Storage	183	110	54	97	37	32	46	28	20
Communications	27	41	24	22	16	20	28	25	25
Energy	68	98	93	92	133	82	75	71	76
Banking & Financial Services	93	90	123	98	96	96	122	86	103
Business & Other Services	219	207	150	206	180	137	163	205	214
Production	**1 072**	**1 072**	**1 032**	**1 000**	**1 078**	**1 215**	**1 167**	**1 227**	**1 128**
Agriculture, Forestry, Fishing	806	827	809	751	847	949	900	908	835
Industry, Mining, Construction	163	147	113	138	129	164	203	202	180
Trade Policies & Tourism	103	98	110	112	102	102	64	117	114
General Environment Protection	309	331	329	368	477	416	406	446	393
Food Assistance	562	750	596	412	496	612	549	629	550
Humanitarian aid	**3 354**	**3 335**	**3 032**	**3 489**	**4 132**	**4 859**	**5 235**	**5 498**	**5 307**
Emergency Response	3 133	3 085	2 782	3 204	3 807	4 518	4 905	4 994	4 981
Reconstruction Relief	91	130	84	77	118	155	113	162	136
Disaster Prevention & Preparedness	130	120	166	208	207	186	218	343	190
Refugees in Donor Countries	**204**	**153**	**169**	**165**	**212**	**204**	**368**	**429**	**443**
Unspecified	**1 574**	**1 664**	**1 059**	**1 004**	**875**	**834**	**745**	**820**	**885**
Total	16 326	16 656	16 257	16 373	17 161	17 094	17 617	17 907	17 455

Source: (OECD, 2020[1]), *Creditor Reporting System* (database), https://stats.oecd.org/Index.aspx?DataSetCode=crs1.

References

OECD (2020), *Creditor Reporting System (database)*,
https://stats.oecd.org/Index.aspx?DataSetCode=crs1.   [1]

Lightning Source UK Ltd.
Milton Keynes UK
UKHW050724070620
364510UK00002B/2